ISBN 978-1-5282-7567-5
PIBN 10928130

1 MONTH OF
FREE
READING

at
www.ForgottenBooks.com

By purchasing this book you are eligible for one month membership to ForgottenBooks.com, giving you unlimited access to our entire collection of over 1,000,000 titles via our web site and mobile apps.

To claim your free month visit:
www.forgottenbooks.com/free928130

Historic, Archive Document

Do not assume content reflects current
scientific knowledge, policies, or practices.

ernational ganizations and ricultural velopment

Kriesberg

International Organizations and Agricultural Development. Martin Kriesberg, Economic Research Service, U.S. Department of Agriculture. Foreign Agricultural Economic Report No. 131.

ABSTRACT

This report describes major international organizations with programs to help low-income countries improve their agriculture and rural sectors. It covers the objectives of multilateral aid organizations, the types of work they do, and the amount of assistance they provide. The publication focuses particularly on activities since the World Food Conference of 1974, but also describes trends in multilateral assistance for the past 12 to 15 years. The report indicates that agricultural programs have gained increased attention among international assistance organizations, and that donor countries have funneled increasing proportions of their total aid through these multilateral organizations.

The report describes the Food and Agriculture Organization, the World Food Council, and other agencies of the United Nations; the World Bank Group; the major regional development banks; and the Organization of American States. Also discussed are the emerging issues and institutional arrangements for multilateral assistance in agriculture.

Keywords: International organizations, Agricultural development, Multilateral assistance.

Washington, D. C. 20250   May 1977

INTERNATIONAL ORGANIZATIONS AND AGRICULTURAL DEVELOPMENT

Martin Kriesberg
Coordinator, International Organization Affairs
Economic Research Service
U.S. Department of Agriculture

ACKNOWLEDGMENTS

Many people and institutions assisted in the preparation of this publication. All cannot be acknowledged here. But assistance from the following should particularly be noted: Pierre Sales, the U.S. Agency for International Development (USAID); Paul Byrnes, Joseph Winder, and John Ferch, Department of State; Ralph W. Phillips, USDA; Fernando Cáceres and Paul Oechsli, Inter-American Development Bank (IDB); Montague Yudelman and Marius Veraart, The World Bank; and Peter Hendry, FAO. I also wish to acknowledge the help of staff members Roger Lewis and Christopher Cannon.

GLOSSARY

AfDB .... African Development Bank
CGFPI .... Consultative Group for Food Production and Investment
CGIAR .... Consultative Group for International Agricultural Research
TAC .... Technical Advisory Committee
CIAP .... Inter-American Committee for the Alliance for Progress
CIEC .... Conference for International Economic Cooperation
ECA .... Economic Commission for Africa
ECAFE............. Economic Commission for Asia and the Far East
ESCAP .... (new name for ECAFE) Economic and Social Commission for Asia and the Pacific
ECLA .... Economic Commission for Latin America
ECOSOC .... Economic and Social Council of the UN
FAO .... Food and Agriculture Organization of the UN
IBRD .... International Bank for Reconstruction and Development (World Bank)
IDA .... International Development Association
IFC .... International Finance Corporation
IDB .... Inter-American Development Bank
SPTF .... Special Progress Trust Fund
FSO .... Fund for Special Operations
IFAD .... International Fund for Agricultural Development
IGAD/LA .... International Group for Agricultural Development/Latin America
IICA (or IAIAS) .... Inter-American Institute for Agricultural Sciences
IMF .... International Monetary Fund
OAS .... Organization of American States
OECD .... Organization for Economic Cooperation and Development
DAC............. Development Assistance Committee
OPEC .... Organization of Petroleum Exporting Countries
P.L. 480 .... Public Law 480 or Food for Peace Program
UN .... United Nations
UNGA .... United Nations General Assembly
UNCTAD .... United Nations Conference on Trade and Development
UNDP.............. United Nations Development Program
UNESCO .... United Nations Educational, Scientific, and Cultural Organization
UNICEF .... United Nations Children's Fund

UNIDO .... United Nations Industrial Development Organization
WFC .... World Food Conference
WFC .... World Food Council
WFP .... World Food Program
WHO .... World Health Organization

CONTENTS

SUMMARY

This report on multilateral assistance in agriculture describes the work of international organizations in the field of food and agriculture supported by the United States. Increased funding has been given to these organizations in recent years, and they have increased the proportion they allocate to programs in food, agriculture, and rural development. This study (an update of the earlier publication, Multilateral Assistance for Agriculture Development, ERS-521) focuses particularly on what has taken place since the World Food Conference of November 1974.

The World Food Conference, and the Seventh Special Session of the United Nations (UN) in September 1975, both dealt with issues affecting the availability of food. The United States played a decisive role in both meetings.

Bilateral and multilateral aid agencies had given increasing attention to the agricultural problems of developing countries in the previous decade. The food crisis of 1973-74 indicated that a greater national and international effort was needed. Three major multilateral aid organizations concerned with food and agricultural development, namely the International Bank for Reconstruction and Development (IBRD or World Bank), the Inter-American Development Bank (IDB), and the Food and Agriculture Organization of the UN (FAO), with its regular and field programs, increased allocations to food and agriculture from less than $200 million a year during 1961-64, to over $600 million during 1970-72. Then commitments were raised to $2.4 billion in 1975, and almost the same level was maintained in 1976.

As a result of the World Food Conference, new institutions were created within the UN system, and older institutions were given broader mandates to help increase food production and improve food security, particularly for vulnerable countries.

The IBRD and the IDB have put major emphasis on projects to improve water supplies and purchase needed production inputs, particularly machinery. In more recent years these two banks have emphasized livestock as well as crops. In the past 3 to 4 years, IBRD and IDB have supported international agricultural research institutions and IBRD has begun a program of socioeconomic research concerning such problems as rural employment and development, protein shortages, and population pressures. FAO has placed its emphasis on training and technical assistance at country levels and now seeks to help with investment studies in farming and agribusiness. FAO has been concerned in recent years about trade problems of developing countries, and the interface between trade policies and development. The international banks and technical assistance agencies, including FAO and the Organization of American States (OAS), have also put increased efforts into country programming and sector analysis.

Important issues have arisen in connection with the increased role of international organizations in worldwide agricultural development and these pose problems for U.S. policy.

While developing countries have pressed for more development aid, they have also asserted claims for a new international economic order. The UN

General Assembly adopted, over opposition of most Western nations, a declaration on a new economic order together with a "charter" on rights and obligations in international economic matters to benefit developing countries. A key question is whether the international organizations will be instruments of development assistance or of fundamental changes in the relationship between industrialized and developing countries.

New ways to overcome differences and to recognize the aspirations of developing countries are being tried. The power of the oil exporting countries is recognized in a new forum, the Conference on International Economic Cooperation, in which the industrialized countries, oil exporting countries, and developing countries share equally in representation. A new International Fund for Agricultural Development, with the same three-way grouping of countries, is being established. A World Food Council has been set up to review and report on programs and progress in food and agricultural activities of other international agencies. UN bodies, including the FAO, are leaning toward more decentralization and developing country aid.

The food crisis of 1973-74 gave added impetus to programs for increasing production in developing countries, but concerns were expressed in some quarters that the drive for higher output would raise problems of equity and benefit the larger producers at the expense of the small farmers and rural workers. International organizations and the countries concerned face issues of resource allocation and development strategy in seeking to benefit the different agricultural groups.

With the increased role of multilateral institutions in providing development assistance, the problem of coordination has grown more complex. At the same time, both donor and recipient governments have become sharper in their concern for more effective deployment of resources. Since the World Food Conference, new institutions have been established with some coordinating responsibilities. But the real issue is who will control and direct the growing flow of resources for food and agricultural development purposes. Among some developing countries, the question is partially answered by the preference for a transfer of resources with a minimum of strings and involvement by donor countries and their institutions. A restructuring of the UN system to make it a more effective economic development instrument for developing country majorities in the General Assembly would shift more control over UN development resources to them.

Difficulty in resolving issues that confront the United States in international forums may cause the United States to turn more frequently to a role of lesser involvement and to abstain from voting on important matters. But this reaction, and the failure of the United States to fully employ its leadership capacity, may, in turn, lead to even more diffusion of purpose and greater departures from the U.S. point of view of the priorities of multilateral agencies. The United States may need to commit itself to greater, rather than less, participation in international organizations.

1. INTRODUCTION

The World Food Conference, convened by the United Nations (UN) in November 1974, and the UN Seventh Special Session held in September 1975 were watersheds in the international effort to deal more effectively with problems of the world's hungry. These two meetings were particularly significant because they dealt with a wide range of issues affecting availability of food for developing countries, and also because the United States played an important role in their achievements.

Both meetings were convened to deal with urgent problems of the developing countries. The United States recognized the need for concerted international action in both, and it advanced important proposals to ameliorate the problems of low-income countries. It was a U.S. proposal that initiated the World Food Conference. The Conference testified that the problems of adequate food supplies for the world's low-income people were not solely problems of farming technology, but involved broad political and economic relationships among nations. The Conference also bore witness to the historic shift from a situation in which U.S. surplus production and stocks of grain would give supply and price stability for much of the world to a situation where such stability could only come about through concerted national and international actions.

The Seventh Special Session of the UN General Assembly (UNGA) was one of several in which the developing countries had pressed demands for a new international economic order. But the session was given a new dimension by U.S. proposals on food and agriculture as well as other economic relationships between industrialized and less developed countries. The speech of the U.S. Secretary of State included these proposals: (1) a doubling of U.S. bilateral aid for the development of food and agriculture in low-income countries, (2) a conditional pledge of $200 million toward a new $1.0 billion International Fund for Agricultural Development, (3) new dialogues on commodities between producer and consumer nations, (4) an increase in the U.S. food aid budgets of 20 percent, and (5) proposals on the establishment of world grain reserves.

U.S. action in both international forums was new evidence of the importance this country gives to discussions on economic development. The United States has been a principal architect of the UN family of agencies concerned with economic development; its financial support for multilateral assistance has increased in the years 1960 to 1975—both in absolute dollars and in comparison with U.S. bilateral assistance. But some thought that the U.S. role in international forums on economic development had become less positive; hence, U.S. actions at the two meetings were taken as a fresh effort at international cooperation with the developing countries.

In the last few years, international institutions have received increasing resources. And the bilateral and multilateral aid agencies have, in turn, allocated an increasing proportion of their resources to the problems of increasing food supplies and improving rural conditions. The food crisis of 1973-74 indicated that a greater national and international effort was needed, and the trend toward greater multilateral aid to agriculture was accelerated.

This study, which updates the earlier publication, Multilateral Assistance for Agricultural Development, focuses particularly on what has taken place since the World Food Conference because these years have been marked by new institutions and new initiatives in the international community. The United States, as well as the international community and its institutions, stands at a new threshold of cooperation or of confrontation. As the strongest economy in the world, and with preeminence in food and agricultural matters, the United States will consciously or unconsciously leave its mark on whatever the international organizations do in the years immediately ahead.

Agricultural Development Activities of International Organizations

There are a large number of intergovernmental organizations involved wholly or partially in world food and agricultural matters. The UN system is the most comprehensive, but it does not emcompass all of these organizations. A recent report of the U.S. Senate Select Committee on Nutrition and Human Needs (46) [1] compiled a list of some 89 international governmental organizations that have an influence on national and international food policies. Included in this listing are UN agencies, international financial or development banks, autonomous intergovernmental commodity groups, specialized technical bodies (for example, the Desert Locust Control Organization for Eastern Africa), and specialized regional bodies (for example, Arab Center for the Study of Arid Zones and Dry Lands). This study encompasses only those organizations that are involved in providing development assistance in food and agriculture for developing countries. Many of the organizations included in this survey began operations as "collegiate" agencies, bringing together like groups of technical personnel. Others were financial institutions that originally served countries at various economic levels, but most have become oriented primarily toward the needs of the developing countries. Except for the discussion beginning on p. 6 regarding development assistance by the oil exporting countries, only organizations officially supported by the United States, and for which available data are reasonably adequate and verifiable by U.S. sources, are included.

Most of the international organizations providing assistance for agricultural development in low-income countries are autonomous organizations associated with the UN system (see fig. 1). These include the Food and Agriculture Organization of the UN (FAO), the organization primarily concerned with the world's agriculture, and the United Nations Development Program (UNDP), which provides some coordination and considerable funding for development activities carried out by FAO and other organizations. The International Bank for Reconstruction and Development

---

[1] Italicized numbers in parentheses refer to items in the Bibliography, p. 132.

THE UNITED NATIONS FAMILY
(A PARTIAL LISTING OF ORGANIZATIONS AND AGENCIES)

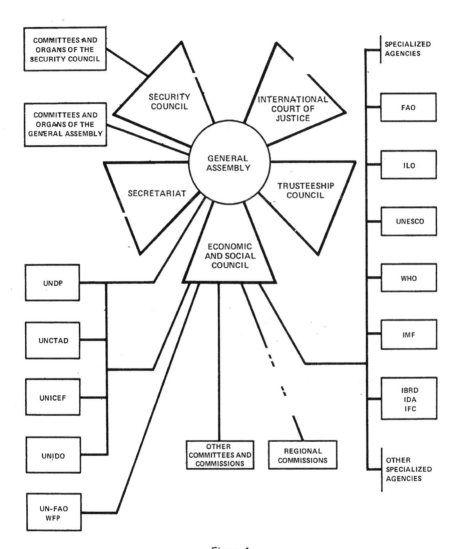

Figure 1

(IBRD or World Bank) and its affiliates, the International Development Association (IDA) and the International Finance Corporation (IFC), are part of the UN family. Most of the international organizations providing economic aid that are affiliated with the UN are linked to it through the United Nations Economic and Social Council (ECOSOC). ECOSOC itself participates in development activities, especially through its Economic Commissions for Asia and the Far East (ECAFE), Africa (ECA), Europe (ECE), and Latin America (ECLA). The United Nations Conference on Trade and Development (UNCTAD) deals, among other things, with the international market side of agricultural development.

A number of organizations were established in the wake of the World Food Conference to deal with various aspects of the food and agriculture problem. One is the World Food Council, a coordinating body providing an overview of what other international organizations are doing; a second is the Consultative Group for Food Production and Investment (CGFPI), and a third is the International Fund for Agricultural Development (IFAD). These new agencies are discussed in Chapter 2. See fig. 3 for their relationship to the UN system.

The Inter-American Development Bank (IDB) and the Asian Development Bank (ADB) are not affiliated with the UN. The African Development Bank (AfDB), though founded under UN sponsorship, operates apart from the UN system. In Latin America, the Organization of American States (OAS) aids the development of agriculture in member states by technical assistance and training activities directly and through its agricultural arm, the Inter-American Institute for Agricultural Sciences (IICA). The agricultural activities of these agencies are included in this report.

This report does not include accounts of organizations concerned less directly with agricultural development, such as the World Health Organization (WHO), International Labor Office (ILO), the United Nations Education, Scientific, and Cultural Organization (UNESCO), nor with the regional economic commissions of the UN.

Trends in Multilateral Assistance

Contributions by OECD/DAC Countries[2]

During the 1960-70 decade, the ratio of multilateral to total aid on the part of the major donor countries formed a "V" curve. About 12 percent of

---

[2]The Organization for Economic Cooperation and Development, made up of industrialized countries, and its Development Assistance Committee (DAC). Member countries include Australia, Austria, Belgium, Canada, Denmark, Finland, France, Germany, Italy, Japan, the Netherlands, Norway, New Zealand, Sweden, Switzerland, United Kingdom, and the United States. Source: Development Cooperation, 1975, p. 132, OECD, Paris.

official development aid went to international organizations in 1960 and 1961; this went down to 6 percent or less in 1963-66 and back up to about 15 percent in 1969. Between 1972 and 1975 the upward trend accelerated as contributions to multilateral organizations increased from 16 percent to 27 percent of donor countries' development assistance (table 1). In 1975, total resource flows from OECD countries reached a new record of $38.8 billion, which exceeded the targeted 1.0 percent of gross national product (GNP) for the first time. Some $13.6 billion of the total was in official development assistance, of which the U.S. contribution exceeded $4.0 billion.

Table 1—Contributions to international organizations as a percentage of total official aid of OECD/DAC countries

Year	Percentage	Year	Percentage
1960	12.1	1968	9.5
1961	12.2	1969	15.8
1962	8.7	1970	16.5
1963	6.1	1971	16.7
1964	6.5	1972	16.6
1965	5.8	1973	24.2
1966	5.2	1974	27.0
1967	10.1	1975	27.6

Within the OECD/DAC countries, the European Economic Community (EEC) carries on a multilateral assistance program through several institutions, principally the European Development Fund and the European Investment Bank. The Fund provides assistance, mostly as grants; its resources are derived from special contributions from member states. The European Investment Bank makes loans on concessional terms; its resources are provided by member states and borrowings on capital markets. [3]

Four phases or resource replenishments have taken place since the EEC program began in 1959. In the third phase, 1970-75, some 900 million units of account (u/a, having a value of about U.S. $1.20 each) were provided for the Fund and 100 million u/a for the Investment Bank. The level of assistance was greatly increased by the fourth replenishment, associated with the Lomé Convention, a new wide-ranging economic aid agreement with 46 countries in Africa, the Caribbean, and the Pacific. Some 3.15 billion u/a were pledged to the Fund and 400 million u/a to the Bank for the period 1975-80. In 1974 and 1975, a significant portion (about 40 percent) of all grant assistance was in the form of food aid. Assistance provided by member states through the EEC Fund and Bank is separate from their respective bilateral programs and

---

[3] Originally, six countries comprised the EEC—France, Germany, Italy, Belgium, Netherlands, and Luxembourg; the United Kingdom, Ireland, and Denmark are also members now and contribute to the EEC multilateral assistance agencies.

participation through other multilateral aid institutions. However, assistance provided through the Fund and the Bank is considered part of official development assistance and is included in the amounts usually aggregated as aid from the OECD/DAC group of countries.

A significant proportion of the assistance provided by the European Development Fund and the European Investment Bank goes for the poorest countries and for rural development. In 1973 and 1974, almost a third of the assistance went to 25 least developed countries. The EEC has always considered aid for rural development to be important and more than one-fourth of the Fund's resources have been assigned to this purpose since 1959. The proportion of aid for rural development has been increasing, and in 1970-75 it averaged over 28 percent of all disbursements. Moreover, almost 95 percent of the aid going to rural development has been in the form of grants.

Most developed countries, after a decline in support for multilateral aid during the middle 1960's, have significantly increased their contributions (table 2).

Table 2–Proportion of official development assistance directed to multilateral organizations

Country	1964-66	1970	1974	Country	1964-66	1970	1974
	Percent				*Percent*		
Norway	66.7	60.2	44.4	Belgium	7.5	22.9	23.4
Sweden	57.5	46.1	41.8	Germany	8.1	22.2	29.0
Denmark	60.5	36.7	44.5	Japan	12.1	18.9	21.8
Netherlands	38.4	21.3	30.5	United Kingdom	10.7	10.7	30.3
Switzerland	32.7	39.1	34.0	Australia	8.0	6.1	9.4
Italy	36.0	47.4	99.9	United States	2.5	12.9	23.6
Austria	30.0	60.3	66.3	France	3.2	10.6	14.1
Canada	21.0	22.7	30.4	Weighted DAC average	6.1	16.5	27.0

Sources: (33) and (34)

The U.S. share of contributions to international organizations more than quadrupled, going from 2.5 percent in 1964-66 to 12.9 percent in 1970, and almost doubling again by 1974 to 23.6 percent. Most of the countries associated with OECD/DAC have increased the percentage of aid going to multinational institutions. The weighted average of all development assistance through multilateral organizations increased from 6.1 percent in 1964-66 to 16.5 percent in 1970 and 27.6 percent in 1975.

Multilateral Assistance by OPEC Countries

As the nations in the Organization of Petroleum Exporting Countries, (OPEC) acquired new wealth and substantial reserves of convertible currencies, questions were raised concerning their contribution toward the economic development of low-income countries. OPEC country efforts to provide development assistance have only recently begun and it is not clear how much of the aid has been for economic development, military, or budgetary support, and how much of the sums publicly announced have actually been disbursed. Three aspects of aid from OPEC countries should be noted. First, the amounts of wealth and reserves among OPEC countries vary greatly; hence their ability to transfer resources to other developing countries also varies. Saudi Arabia, Kuwait, Qatar, and the United Arab Emirates, with relatively small populations and large earnings, and to a lesser extent Iran and Venezuela are in a position to make significant contributions. Other OPEC countries, such as Indonesia and Nigeria, do not have large capital reserves. Second, most of the grant or concessional aid that has been provided thus far has been directed toward Arab countries and appears to be for budgetary support purposes. Third, most of the resources that have been provided through existing international organizations have been by purchases of bonds marketed by the development banks, which carry good interest rates and guarantees by the industrialized countries.

Multilateral aid has been a small part of the total aid announced by OPEC countries. In 1974 concessional development assistance disbursed by OPEC countries was about $2.5 billion for all purposes. Of this sum about $350 million, or 14 percent, was disbursed through multilateral institutions. It is not known what proportion of this money was for food and agricultural projects in recipient countries. In 1975 concessional assistance disbursed by OPEC countries was about $2.7 billion, with about $560 million going through multilateral institutions. Most of the money contributed to multilateral agencies went to newly established regional Arab institutions. Table 3 lists the multilateral institutions receiving support from OPEC countries and the amount of commitments and disbursements in 1974 and 1975.

In 1976 an $800 million special fund with contributions from 11 OPEC countries was established. It is to provide very concessional loans, particularly for some 40 countries identified by the UN as most in need. The OPEC ministers indicated that $400 million of this was earmarked as an OPEC contribution to the International Fund for Agricultural Development (IFAD).

Trends in Program Commitments by International Organizations

In all the multilateral institutions supported by the United States and other OECD/DAC countries, higher priority is being given to agriculture and rural development. The UNDP, IBRD, and IDB allocated greatly increased funds for agricultural projects during the late 1960's and early 1970's. As shown in table 4 and figure 2, agricultural allocations by these three multilateral aid organizations and the FAO grew from $330 million in 1967-68 to about $2.4 billion in 1975, and almost the same level was maintained in 1976. During 1971 and 1972, when problems of food supplies seemed less urgent, the proportion of funding going to agricultural projects

Table 3—OPEC assistance through multilateral organizations,
1974 and 1975[1]

Multilateral organization	Commitments		Disbursements	
	1974	1975	1974	1975
	Million dollars			
African Development Bank and Fund	33	27	31	24
Arab Fund for Economic and Social Development	38	44	38	44
OAPEC[2] Special Account	78	62	78	5
Special Arab Fund for Africa	160	–	60	100
Arab Bank for Economic Development in Africa	100	100		80
Islamic Development Bank	140	143		142
Islamic Solidarity Fund	13	2	–	6
Caribbean Development Bank	10	–	10	–
UN Special Acct. & UN Agencies	170	125	120	107
IDA and IBRD[3]	11	71	9	39
Other	8	25	1	13
Total	761	599	347	560

– = No funding action reported

[1] See (35) p. 5, and "Recent Development Initiatives," p. 7. OECD Observer, Jan-Feb., 1976. Also, OECD Document, the Aid Programs of OPEC Members, Nov. 1976.

[2] Organization of Arab Petroleum Exporting Countries.

[3] IBRD's Third Window is included for 1975.

declined. Then, as the situation worsened precipitously, national governments and international institutions took urgent action to increase the flow of resources again for food and agriculture programs.

The increased flows have been hurt somewhat by inflation. In 1971 contributions to agriculture were $664 million. In 1973 contributions reached $1.29 billion, in 1974 they reached $1.37 billion, and in 1975, $2.44 billion. But in terms of 1971 dollars, we get: 1973, $924 million; 1974, $892 million; and 1975, $1.417 billion.[4]

Multilateral aid organizations are directing increased attention to problems of the least developed among the developing countries and the poorest sectors of the population within them. Existing programs are being reexamined and a search is underway for new programs to reach these groups which, thus far, have participated little in the improved economic conditions of the 1960's and 1970's.

Multilateral organizations have tended to broaden the scope of their programs. Thus, the international lending institutions, such as the World Bank

[4] World Bank, Technical Note on Deflators, see M76-803, Nov. 29, 1976.

Table 4—Agricultural funding by international organizations, 2-year average 1963-70, annual 1971-76

Organization/category	1963-64	1965-66	1967-68	1969-70	1971	1972	1973	1974	1975	1976
					Million dollars					
IBRD/IDA[1]	52.0	159.0	130.0	397.9	419.2	436.3	937.7	955.9	1,857.5	1,627.6[3]
IDB/FSO[1]	70.2	70.8	110.0	219.3	93.2	130.0	187.0	228.0	332.0	450.0[3]
FAO/UNDP[2]	49.3	70.6	92.2	120.2	151.6	157.7	165.2	185.2	254.1	278.0[3]
Total agricultural funding	171.5	300.4	332.2	737.4	664.0	724.0	1,289.9	1,369.1	2,443.6	2,355.6
Total, all funding	1,229	1,681	1,598	2,743	3,308	3,930	4,454	5,610	7,525	8,460.4
Agricultural funding as percent of total	14	18	21	27	20	18	29	24	32	28

[1] IBRD and IDB, as financial institutions, report funding in terms of program activities; the figures here do not include their administrative costs. IBRD figures are for fiscal years.

[2] FAO's regular budget, UNDP funds allocated to FAO, and other resources provided for FAO's work.

[3] Estimate. (The IBRD/IDA figure is for the fiscal year ending June 30, 1976.)

9

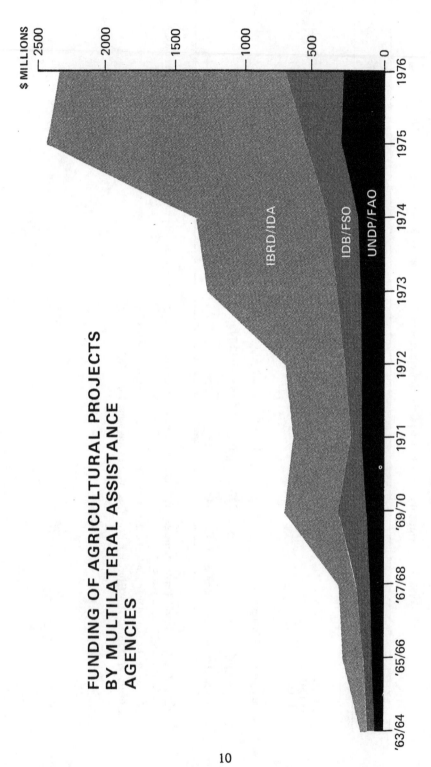

FUNDING OF AGRICULTURAL PROJECTS
BY MULTILATERAL ASSISTANCE
AGENCIES

$ MILLIONS

IBRD/IDA

IDB/FSO

UNDP/FAO

Figure 2

10

and the Inter-American Development Bank, have included more technical assistance in their operations. FAO, which is a technical assistance organization in the agricultural, fisheries, and forestry fields, has working arrangements with financial institutions to provide capital assistance components for some of its projects, and it plans to use its technical staff to identify new investment opportunities for agriculture in developing countries.

The United States and the International Organizations

U.S. Contributions to Multinational Development Organizations

The principal multinational organizations to which the United States has contributed are the United Nations and its specialized agencies and the international development banks. Most U.S. contributions have been in amounts and at times determined in concert with other member countries. To a large extent, contributions are related to the countries' relative ability to pay. The United States has also made voluntary contributions to the international finance institutions, but most of the support has been through capital subscriptions, including provisions for callable capital resources. The callable capital is not paid in but provides the guarantee which permits development banks to borrow monies at favorable rates in the commercial money markets.

The U.S. approach in contributing to multinational aid organizations has been characterized by several considerations. First, the United States has moved to have more of its overall economic and humanitarian assistance channeled through the international institutions. Second, it has sought to strengthen the administrative and operational effectiveness of these organizations so that the United States and the recipient countries obtain increased value for the money expended. Third, the United States has urged the international organizations to give priority in their aid to the most needy countries and population groups within them. Fourth, the United States has sought to have its contributions make up a smaller part of the total development programs of the international organizations by encouraging other developed countries (and developing countries with large reserves) to carry a greater share of the burden.

As indicated previously, U.S. contributions to international organizations have increased significantly over the past decade and now run about 30 percent of its total official development assistance. Table 5 indicates the trend of U.S. bilateral and multilateral assistance for the 13-year period, fiscal 1964-76. In multilateral assistance the portions of the AID and USDA P.L. 480 funds allocated to multilateral institutions have been subtracted from the bilateral figures and included along with direct appropriations to multilateral agencies.

U.S. appropriations for the development banks include monies for capital subscriptions and for concessional fund operations. U.S. appropriations for

11

Table 5—U.S. bilateral and multilateral assistance, 2-year averages to 1973, annual for 1974-76

Category	FY 1964-65	FY 1966-67	FY 1968-69	FY 1970-71	FY 1972-73	FY 1974	FY 1975	FY 1976
				Million dollars				
Bilateral assistance								
USAID (economic, humanitarian, and support assistance)	1,985.0	1,953.0	1,726.0	1,539.8	1,580.7	1,452.3	1,898.1	2,767.1
P.L. 480 food aid (expenditures)	2,239.7	1,790.5	1,259.0	1,093.0	1,039.0	849.0	1,076.0	964.0
Peace Corps	80.8	108.9	103.6	87.9	77.8	76.9	77.6	81.0
Total	4,305.5	3,852.4	3,088.6	2,720.7	2,697.5	2,378.2	3,051.7	3,812.1
Multilateral assistance								
Asian Development Bank	–	70.1	10.5	20.0	–	50.0	74.1	120.6
Inter-American Development Bank[1]	318.5	352.9	402.9	390.5	315.1	418.4	225.0	440.0
World Bank[2]	61.7	104.0	132.0	160.0	221.5	320.0	320.0	375.0
UN and UN agencies[3]	60.7	72.6	87.4	101.4	130.2	141.5	142.4	190.0
Regional organizations[4]	23.3	27.5	29.2	36.6	45.8	56.7	59.4	66.1
Special voluntary programs[5]	194.4	224.6	189.3	233.6	345.2	284.1	335.7	546.2
Total	658.6	851.7	851.3	942.1	1,057.8	1,270.7	1,156.6	1,737.9
Total foreign assistance	4,964.1	4,704.1	3,939.9	3,662.8	3,755.3	3,648.9	4,208.3	5,550.0
				Percent				
Percent multilateral	13.3	18.1	21.6	25.7	28.2	34.8	27.5	31.3

Sources: AID: Total program availability from ... Presentation, Reports ..., ... Office of Financial ... Agent, P.L. 480: ASCS/USDA; ... do not ... transportation costs. Development banks: Annual Reports, UN and UN agencies, regional organizations, and ... voluntary ...: 1964–1976, communication from the Secretary of State transmitting the Annual Report o U.S. Contributions to International Organizations, Washington; House Document No. 94-333 and preceding annual ... in 1974 and 976.

The IDB operates o a calendar-year ... but the figures used ... are FY appropriations during the respective calendar ...; FY 1973 figures ... $225 million for repl ... of the FSO and $193.4 ... of ordinary capital.

[2] The World Bank figures for 1964–71 are for r ... of IDA; for 1972-73, a portion is also for ... commitments to the World Bank prior to the 1964 figures ... the U.S. ... of $320 millio o ... ... and $312 million in ... the" ... subscribed to when the Bank was established.

[3] Figures for the UN agency ... are for ... ... for the regular operations of the UN and its associated organizations.

... the regional organizations ... ... of the inter-American ...

[5] The ... voluntary ... ... contributions for the UNDP, WFP, WHO, and also the ... refugee programs, Special voluntary ... ... shw a ... ... for the ... 1972-73, owing to the Bangladesh relief ... and for ... stricken countries of Africa; in 1 976 the ... ... is ... for by $200 million ... for IFAD.

regular operations of such organizations as FAO, UNESCO, UNCTAD, and UNICEF are also included. Two-year averages are used in the table from 1964 to 1973 to reduce chance year-to-year fluctuations. Yearly totals are used for 1974 to 1976 to allow for annual comparison. The increased level of bilateral aid in fiscal year 1975 and 1976 is associated with expanded support assistance in the Middle East.

Over the years, as the proportion of assistance provided by other industrialized countries has increased, the U.S. share of total multilateral aid has declined (see table 6). The U.S. contribution to FAO was 25 percent when the organization was first established in 1945; it rose to 32.5 percent in 1958-61, dropped to 31.5 percent during 1972-73, and is now again at 25 percent. The U.S. contribution to the UNDP during 1972-75 was about 30 percent of total contributions, down from almost 40 percent in previous years.

Table 6—U.S. share of total funding of selected international
financial organizations, 1960-75

Organization	1960	1965	1968	1970	1975
			Percent		
IBRD	32.9	29.3	27.7	27.4	25.34
IBRD/IDA	43.1	41.6	40.0	39.5	37.13
IDB	43.0	43.0	42.8	42.5	40.39
IDB/FSO	91.4	83.3	75.0	66.7	69.18
ADB	–	–	20.6	19.9	16.63

U.S. Government Agencies and the International Organizations

Within the executive branch of the U.S. Government, the Department of State has overall responsibility for U.S. relations with multinational organizations. Liaison with the international finance institutions such as IBRD and IDB is delegated to the Treasury Department, and the Department of Agriculture coordinates participation with FAO (46). In each of these departments an assistant secretary concerned with international affairs provides leadership. The Treasury Department operates through an interagency committee, the National Advisory Council on International Monetary and Financial Policies (NAC), which includes representatives of AID, the Export-Import Bank, the Federal Reserve Bank, and the Departments of State, Commerce, and Agriculture, as well as other agencies having an interest in international economic affairs. The NAC submits an annual report to the President and the Congress. In providing liaison for FAO, the Department of Agriculture works through an interagency committee which has representatives from AID, the Departments of Commerce and Interior, and agencies of other departments concerned with international agriculture, fisheries, and forestry. The two committees and the

13

agencies represented are responsible for formulating U.S. policy on programs and operations of the multilateral agencies. The Department of State provides leadership and liaison with the UN General Assembly and the UNDP, but it delegates technical responsibility for other technical UN bodies, such as the ILO and WHO, to the appropriate U.S. agency, such as the Department of Labor or the Department of Health, Education, and Welfare.

In each department with delegated responsibility, a few people devote most of their time to the activity and draw upon others as needed from their agency and other relevant agencies for drafting U.S. position papers and participating in technical meetings or in meetings of the governing bodies. As UN specialized organizations have become the scene of political as well as technical debates, with issues being carried over from debates in the UN General Assembly, the need for continuity and political sensitivity on the part of U.S. representatives to the FAO, the World Food Council, and other UN agencies becomes more evident.

Because world food and agriculture problems have an impact on U.S. domestic as well as foreign policies and on nonagricultural as well as agricultural sectors, U.S. agencies with several different missions and constituencies are involved in shaping U.S. policies in international agriculture. For example, the Department of Agriculture has a special interest in helping expand exports of agricultural commodities; the Treasury Department has a concern with balance of payments and the cost of food in the United States; and the Department of State has a primary interest in how international agricultural policies affect U.S. foreign policy objectives. To assure involvement of the different U.S. agencies and interests in this process, additional coordinating mechanisms have been recently established.

Under provisions of the U.S. Foreign Assistance Act, as amended in 1974, the Development Coordination Committee was established. This committee is chaired by the Administrator of USAID, and has representatives from the Departments of Agriculture, State, Treasury, Labor, and Commerce, as well as the Export-Import Bank, the Office of Management and Budget, the National Security Council, and others. The Development Coordination Committee is responsible for U.S. policies affecting the development of low-income countries. It publishes an annual report to the Congress on development events and issues. The Council of International Economic Policy and the Agricultural Policy Committee are two other interagency bodies concerned with U.S. policies on world food and agricultural matters. The latter, established by the President in March 1976, includes the work of *ad hoc* committees established earlier to deal with American grain sales to the Soviet Union and to follow up on actions stemming from the World Food Conference.

2. WORLD FOOD CONFERENCE AND NEW INTERNATIONAL INSTITUTIONS

The World Food Conference

The World Food Conference was convened by the UN General Assembly and held in Rome, November 5-16, 1974. It was a historic meeting of ministers. Proposals for such a conference had been formally made by nonaligned governments meeting in Algiers September 5-9, 1973, and also by the U.S. Secretary of State in an address to the UN General Assembly on the 24th of that month. The proposal was acted on promptly by the UN bodies involved.

The UN was responding to the serious food situation that confronted the world as a result of widespread crop failures in 1973 among industrialized as well as less developed countries. Particularly hard hit were the developing countries who were dependent on imports for their food supplies but who lacked the means to pay for both higher priced oil as well as foodstuffs. Unlike previous international meetings held in connection with food and agriculture, the 1974 Conference candidly recognized that the problems to be overcome were less technical than political and economic, and that firmer political wills were needed to commit the increased resources and make the policy decisions essential for a more rapid increase in food production.

Government representatives at the Conference gave expression to a common concern and responsibility for alleviating the world food situation, and made commitments which laid the foundation for actions at both national and international levels since the meeting. The Conference agreed upon a "Universal Declaration on the Eradication of Hunger and Malnutrition" which embodied the concerns and aspirations of the delegates and put the problem in the context of broader international economic relations. The Conference also agreed on some 20 resolutions which addressed various problems of food and agriculture—particularly as they pertained to the needs of developing countries. These resolutions were adopted by the UN General Assembly in December 1974, thereby adding its weight to the Conference conclusions and call for action.

Conference Resolutions

Prior to the meeting of ministers at the World Food Conference, there had been several preparatory meetings of representative governments at which an agenda and an agreed conference product were negotiated. At the third preparatory session, some 10 operative resolutions were agreed upon and these became the basis for the more extensive resolutions adopted at the final plenary meeting of the Conference. In its early deliberations, the Conference decided to establish three working committees to draft language for the resolutions. The resolutions adopted by the Conference were in the following areas:

‛Food production. Recommendations on food production were as follows:

• In order to solve the food problem, highest priority should be given to policies and programs for increasing food production and improving food utilization in developing countries; food production and food utilization objectives, targets, and policies, for the short, medium, and long term should be formulated with full participation of producers, their families, and farmers' and fishermen's organizations; agrarian reforms and adequate supporting services, credit facilities, and incentives should be developed; external assistance should be increased and an International Fund for Agricultural Development set up (Resolution I).

• Governments should organize, activate, and assist the rural population for participation in integrated rural development. Governments should also promote the development of cooperative organizations and other associations for the mass of farmers and rural workers—generating greater self-reliance and self-sufficiency. Price relationships should be set which would increase incentives and incomes. International agencies should review their criteria for assistance for integrated rural development, giving greater importance to social criteria (Resolution II).

• The FAO Commission on Fertilizer should undertake an authoritative analysis of the long-term fertilizer supply and demand situation; also, increased support should be given to international fertilizer programs. Financial and technical assistance, and technology and equipment on favorable terms should be provided to build required additional fertilizer production capacities in appropriate developing countries that possess natural resources, or where specific local factors justify such investments (Resolution III).

• Agricultural research, training, and extension programs should be intensified at national and international levels. Basic and applied research should, in particular, be concerned with the impact of climate, weather, and their variability on agricultural production and with the application of meteorological information and knowledge in planning land use. The resources of the Consultative Group on International Agricultural Research should be substantially enlarged (Resolution IV).

• Policies and programs for improving nutrition should be strengthened by national governments and international organizations (Resolution V).

• A world soil chart and land capability assessment study should be undertaken (Resolution VI); water management schemes should be intensified (Resolution VII); women's rights and responsibilities in the battle against world hunger should be promoted (Resolution VIII); rational long-term population policies should be supported (Resolution IX); and military expenditures should be reduced to allow increased outlays for increasing food production (Resolution XIV).

On the issue of providing more financing for increased food production in developing countries, a target of $5 billion a year in external assistance was formulated. But except for the related provision calling for the establishment of a new international agricultural development fund, there was no indication of how the added flow of resources might come about. Although there were

16

statements on the primary responsibility of the developing countries themselves, there was no indication how they might increase the allocation of internal resources for food and agricultural development, or to what extent these countries had the absorptive capacity for substantial increases of external funds.

Food security. Among the principal recommendations on food security were these:

- A Global Information and Early Warning System on Food and Agriculture, operated and supervised by FAO, should be established (Resolution XVI). The information thus collected should be fully analyzed and disseminated periodically to all participating governments and for their exclusive use. The World Meteorological Organization should also provide regular assessments of current and recent weather to identify changes in patterns, investigate weather/crop relationships, and encourage investigations on the probability of adverse weather conditions occurring in various agricultural areas. In the debate on the resolution, the Soviet Union and the People's Republic of China indicated their sovereign rights would be infringed by making public information on food supplies; hence, they would not agree to release "confidential" data on supplies, stocks, prices, and trade of foodstuffs.

- The International Undertaking on World Food Security, which had earlier been proposed by FAO, should be established and supported by all governments (Resolution XVII). The Undertaking carried the introductory statement that it is the common responsibility of the entire international community for evolving policies and arrangements designed to ensure world food security and, in particular, to maintain adequate regional and national stocks. The importance of participation of all producing and consuming countries in the FAO Undertaking was stressed. The FAO Undertaking commits governments to "adopt policies concerning cereals . . . which would result in maintaining a minimum safe level of basic cereal stocks for the world as a whole," to "establish stock targets . . . at least at the level necessary for ensuring continuity of supply including provision for emergencies; to replenish stocks as soon as feasible." In periods of shortages, stocks "in excess of minimum safe levels for domestic needs" should be made available for export "on reasonable terms."

The need for improved policies and programs for food aid was expressed in Resolution XVII. The resolution notes there is a need for continuity and a minimum level of food aid in physical terms. Forward planning and commitments were urged with 10 million tons of grain a year cited as a target. Multilateral and bilateral programs should be coordinated through the World Food Program's Intergovernmental Committee, and emergency stocks should be earmarked.

Trade in foodstuffs. Among the provisions on which some consensus was reached were that trade should be liberalized, speculative practices should be prevented, and world markets stabilized. There was need for measures to assure the poorer sectors of rural populations (in exporting developing countries) of a reasonable share in the opportunities and benefits offered by trade expansion. International arrangements are cited as a means for dealing with the problem of stabilizing world markets, particularly for foodstuffs.

International agricultural adjustments were proposed that might enable and facilitate, to the extent possible, the expansion of food and agricultural imports from developing countries in competition with domestic production of developed countries (Resolution XIX).

The Conference also called for a number of new organizations and institutional arrangements to assure more effective followup to the substantive resolutions and to coordinate many old and new activities. The resolutions for new institutions reflected the efforts of many developing countries to gain more purposeful action through the UN system and some resistance by industrial countries and others to the establishment of additional international organizations.

Many of the followup actions were delegated to existing international institutions in line with their ongoing programs. In Resolution XXII, the Conference called for three new institutions—a World Food Council, an International Fund for Agricultural Development (described in a separate Resolution XIII), and a Consultative Group on Food Production and Investment. These new institutions are described in the following pages.

Figure 3 indicates the relationships of these three new international institutions to other organizations of the UN system concerned with food and agricultural development. The chart also indicates some of the institutional arrangements within older organizations, such as FAO, to assure effective followup to proposals made by the Conference.

World Food Council

The Conference agreed to establish a World Food Council, entrusting it with followup and coordinating responsibilities. Meeting in December 1974, the UN General Assembly adopted Resolution XXII of the World Food Conference with its provisions that the Council functions would include:

(1) Periodic reviews of major problems and policy issues affecting the world food situation;

(2) Periodic reviews of steps being proposed or taken to resolve the problem by governments, by the United Nations system, and its regional organizations;

(3) Recommendation of remedial action as appropriate to resolve these problems;

(4) Coordination of relevant UN bodies and agencies dealing with food problems, giving special attention to the problems of the least developed and most seriously affected countries;

(5) Maintaining contacts with, receiving reports from, giving advice to, and making recommendations to UN bodies and agencies with regard to the formulation and followup of world food policies, and full cooperation with regional bodies to formulate and follow up policies approved by the Council.

The World Food Council meets at the ministerial level to engender appropriate political weight to its deliberations and decisions. Thus, the Council was designated as the highest institution on world food problems in the UN system, with responsibilities that transcend near-term followup activities of the World Food Conference.

(Partial Listing)

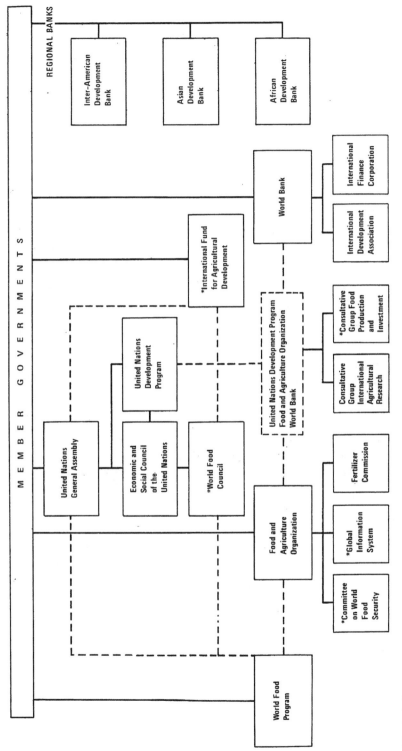

Figure 3

* New Institutions.

Organization and Operations

When the General Assembly accepted the resolution to create the World Food Council it also accepted nominations of ECOSOC for the 36 countries which would initially comprise the new body. They were as follows: nine members from African states—Chad, Egypt, Gabon, Guinea, Kenya, Libya, Mali, Togo, and Zambia; eight members from Asian states—Bangladesh, India, Indonesia, Iran, Iraq, Japan, Pakistan, Sri Lanka; seven members from Latin Amercan states—Argentina, Colombia, Cuba, Guatemala, Mexico, Trinidad and Tobago, and Venezuela; four members from the socialist states of Eastern Europe—Hungary, Romania, Yugoslavia, and the USSR; and eight members from Western Europe and other states—Australia, Canada, France, Germany, Italy, Sweden, United Kingdom, and the United States. Membership will be rotated, with 12 states serving initially for 1 year, 12 for 2 years, and 12 for 3 years, with reelection possible.

Since coming into being, the World Food Council has met twice at the ministerial level—in June of 1975 and again in June of 1976. A third meeting is scheduled for June of 1977. The very breadth of the Council's mandate led to efforts, in its first two meetings, to clarify the Council's authority and focus the work of its Secretariat. Member countries have been divided as to how much authority the Council should have to oversee and provide direction to other international bodies concerned with food and agricultural problems. In general, developing countries sought a Council with more authority, while industrialized countries favored a more deliberative body for better coordination of international agencies promoting food and agricultural development.

The Secretariat of the Council is small, and member countries agree that a new international bureaucracy should not be created. The Council is not an operating agency, but rather a forum and mechanism for reviewing the work of other international organizations with operating programs. The executive director of the Council is appointed by the UN Secretary General in consultation with FAO and other international institutions. The Secretariat also includes a deputy and an assistant director, together with a small staff. The terms of the appointments have not been fixed thus far. The Council has relied on FAO, UNDP, and the World Bank for personnel support during its first year's operation.

At the first meeting of the World Food Council, a president was elected and given authority to represent the Council at the political level. This arrangement continued through the second meeting of the Council and there is some ambiguity as to the spheres of authority and responsibility of the Council's executive director and of its president.

To expedite the work of the Council, the Secretariat prepares papers on the principal agenda items to be considered. The Council Secretariat receives reports on programs and policies of UN agencies concerned with and bearing on world food problems. These, together with data and reports, particularly from FAO, IBRD, and the UNDP, provide the raw material for its studies. However, the analyses made and the papers prepared for the Council meetings are drafted specifically for that body. Preparatory committees representing the member nations of the Council meet several weeks prior to the ministers' sessions, review the Secretariat's draft papers, and define the issues which should be considered by the Council at the ministerial level. Reports of the Council's deliberations and recommendations are prepared by the Secretariat and transmitted in the name of the World Food Council to the General Assembly through the UN's Economic and Social Council for information or further action.

Program of Work

The Secretariat sees the Council as providing a mechanism for overall, integrated, and continuing coordination and followup of policies concerning food production, nutrition, food security, food trade, and food aid. To do this, the Secretariat feels that it must:

a) Mobilize additional resources for the objectives and targets approved by the World Food Conference;

b) Persuade governments to develop the political will required to undertake policy actions which are necessary for solving their food problems at the national and international levels; and

c) Promote the required coordination in the work of the agencies and organizations, international and regional, multilateral and bilateral, that directly or indirectly affect the ultimate solution of the world food problem.[1]

In each of these areas, the role of the Council is seen as selective and complementary to the programs and activities of other international bodies, particularly FAO, the development banks, and the UNDP.

Three of the major components of an overall food strategy, namely food production, food security, and food aid, were on the agenda of the Council at its second session. On the issue of food production, the Council agreed that accelerating production in developing countries was of highest priority. Assessment of progress toward production targets and identification of what else might be done to overcome obstacles and constraints on production will likely be continuing subjects on the Council's agenda. The Secretariat placed a number of proposals before the Council at its second session so that delegates might decide on a course of action for their own efforts and the Secretariat's. While there was substantial agreement on the actions proposed in the Secretariat's paper, the second session of the Council did not adopt the proposals as outlined. A principal point of difference among Council members was in quantifying and setting new targets for resource transfers to developing countries.

A second major component of an overall food strategy, world food security, has been interpreted differently in different forums and by different

---

[1]Executive Director's note for the Council meeting in June 1976.

21

countries. At its first session, the Council affirmed its responsibility to follow up on implementation of the International Undertaking on World Food Security. At the second session the Council sought to focus on the discussions and consultations regarding food security and reserves of food grain which were taking place in other international forums. The Council did not reach a consensus on what it should do to further the processes already underway or whether it should try some other approaches.

The third important element to an overall food strategy is seen as improved policies for food aid—relating it to production, nutrition, and development objectives of recipient countries. While most members agreed on the need to improve food aid along these lines, there was a lack of consensus at the second meeting on what specific actions the Council should take, for itself or vis-a-vis other international bodies.

Two other elements of an overall world food strategy are planned for the agenda of the third Council meeting, namely food trade and nutrition.[2]

On international food trade, the Council Secretariat looks to World Food Conference Resolution XIX, which called for governments to "cooperate in promoting a steady and increasing expansion and liberalization of world trade with special reference to food products...taking into account the specific trade problems of developing countries." Although discussions on trade in agricultural commodities, including foodstuffs, are going on in a number of other international forums, the Council Secretariat sees the need to consider food trade from the perspective of "expanding international trade in foodstuffs, providing developing countries with a greater and more secure access to markets, and speeding up the removal of specific trade impediments to the expansion of food production in developing countries."

On nutrition, the Council Secretariat takes its cues from Resolution V of the World Food Conference which deals specifically with policies and programs to improve nutrition, and from the declaration made then to seek the elimination of hunger and malnutrition from the world within the next decade. Resolution V includes references to special feeding programs for children and other vulnerable groups, a global nutrition surveillance system to monitor the food and nutrition conditions of disadvantaged groups of the population, and assistance to governments for developing intersectoral food and nutritional plans. Again, work on improving nutrition is underway in several international bodies, and the Council Secretariat will seek to determine where the gaps and constraints are and what and where more might be done to speed the work and make the efforts more effective.

At its first session, the Council directed the Secretariat to "begin work on a realistic and practical assessment to determine the feasibility and implications of abolishing hunger and malnutrition in a decade" in line with the World Food Conference declaration. The Secretariat may submit a preliminary analysis on this for consideration at the third meeting of the Council.

---

[2]Report of the World Food Council, June 24, 1976, including the work of the preparatory meeting.

Council Resources

The World Food Council provides neither capital nor technical assistance to member nations; hence, it operates with only a small administrative budget. In its first year of operation, the Council was financed largely by allocations from IBRD, FAO, and UNDP. It also received personnel on loan from these organizations, and salaries were partially covered by them. The program of work envisaged by the Secretariat on behalf of the Council members and the international community at large requires a somewhat larger technical staff and a firmer financial base than it has had for the past year. The Secretariat indicated at the second meeting of the Council it would seek the needed financial and personnel resources within the framework of the UN budget system. At the 31st UN General Assembly the Council was voted its own funds for operations during 1977.

International Fund For Agricultural Development

It had been agreed at the World Food Conference that developing countries would need increased resources if their production of food was to be accelerated. The Conference, in Resolution XIII, proposed the establishment of a new international fund to finance agricultural development projects, primarily for food in the developing countries. The proposal had first been made by a group of OPEC countries which indicated they would share the funding with the industrialized countries. Most industrialized countries initially questioned the idea, but later accepted it.

The new Fund was to embody a number of principles and provisions not found in existing financial institutions, as suggested in Resolution XIII and the discussions on it during the World Food Conference:

• The Fund would be administered by its own governing board consisting of representatives of contributing developed countries, contributing developing countries (the OPEC group), and potential recipient countries. There was to be "equitable" distribution of representation among the three categories of countries. This was interpreted as equal voting power among the three groups and, in early discussions, the group of oil exporting countries indicated they would match the contribution of the industrialized countries.

• Disbursements from the Fund would be carried out through existing international and/or regional institutions in accordance with regulations and criteria to be established by the Fund's governing board.

• The Secretary General of the United Nations was responsible for bringing the Fund into being and was requested to call a meeting of "interested countries" representing the three categories of countries to work out details. Responsibility for handling the meetings and providing a Secretariat was delegated to the World Food Council.

• Negotiations for the Fund would be initiated when the Secretary General determined, after consultations with countries willing to contribute

23

to the Fund, that it held promise of generating substantial additional resources for assistance to developing countries and that its operations had a reasonable prospect of continuity.

The Fund's Articles of Agreement

The Secretary General called the first meeting of interested governments in April 1975 at Geneva. At that session he came to the conclusion that there were good possibilities that the Fund could be established. Accordingly, a series of working group meetings were scheduled to formulate the Articles of Agreement and to begin informal indications of the amounts that each contributing country would pledge.

At the working group meeting in September 1975, the U.S. representative reported the Secretary of State's declaration that the United States would seek an appropriation of $200 million toward a total Fund of $1 billion, in which there would be equitable burden sharing between the oil exporting countries (OPEC) and the industrialized countries. This statement of support by the United States, though conditional, signaled the beginning of earnest negotiations.

At a meeting of interested governments held in Rome, January 28-February 6, 1976, the Articles of Agreement were finally worked out and recommended to member governments for adoption. The Articles were approved by plenipotentiaries at a meeting held in May 1976.

Among the important provisions in the Articles are the following:[3]

Purpose of the fund. "... to mobilize additional resources to be made available on concessional terms for agricultural development in developing member states ... the Fund shall provide financing primarily for projects and programs specifically designed to introduce, expand, or improve food production systems and to strengthen related policies and institutions ... taking into consideration the need to increase food production in the poorest food-deficit countries; the potential for increasing production in other developing countries; and the importance of improving the nutritional level of the poorest populations. ..."

Membership. There will be three categories of members: developed donor countries, developing donor countries (members of OPEC), and developing countries—who may or may not make contributions and who may make their contributions in convertible or in local currencies.

Organization and management. The Fund will have a Governing Council, an Executive Board, and a small staff for carrying out its operations. The Governing Council will be comprised of representatives of all member countries; the Executive Board of 18 representatives will be elected by the Council. Voting power within the two governing bodies will be divided

---

[3]Articles of Agreement as recorded in the official report on the Fund issued by the World Food Council after the meeting of plenipotentiaries in May 1976.

equally among each of the three categories of members. And within each category, voting power will be determined by the member states of each category.

Operations. Within policy guidelines set by the Articles of Agreement and the Governing Council, decisions on projects and programs will be made by the Executive Board. "Usually the services of international institutions will be used for program and project appraisals" and "the Fund shall entrust the administration of loans, their disbursement and supervision, to competent international institutions."

Relations with the UN. The Fund will seek a relationship with the UN as one of its specialized agencies.

Coming into force. Article XIII of the Agreement carries the provision that the Articles shall be open to signature when $1 billion (equivalent of U.S. dollars) is pledged by the two groups of donor countries making their contributions in convertible currencies. Also, the Fund may begin operations when $750 million of the total has been deposited to its account.

Although the Articles of Agreement do not contain language on the relative level of contributions as between the two groups of donor countries, there had been some expectation of rough parity between the two groups. At the meeting of plenipotentiaries convened in May 1976, pledges of approximately $930 million were received. Of this sum, the industrialized countries pledged some $520 million and the oil exporting countries pledged $400 million. Developing countries pledged some $10 million in convertible currencies. Since the target $1 billion in pledges had not been reached, the Articles of Agreement were not opened for signature. Nevertheless, a preparatory commission was established to make administrative arrangements for the Fund's operation as soon as final agreement on pledges would be reached. The UN Secretary General was again asked to use his good offices to achieve such agreement. Provisionally, the Fund is to be located in Rome and the preparatory commission is making administrative arrangements for the procurement of space and secretariat services there. A second preparatory commission meeting was held in December 1976. At that time, pledges were at hand indicating that the target of $1 billion was attained. The United States signed the Articles of Agreement on December 22, 1976. A strategy for food and agricultural development was later tabled as a basis for the Fund's operations.

Consultative Group On Food Production and Investment

Resolution XXII of the World Food Conference called for the establishment of a new international body whose principal functions would be to (1) encourage larger external flows of resources for food production in developing countries, (2) coordinate activities of various donors, and (3) ensure more effective use of available resources. The Consultative Group on Food Production and Investment (CGFPI) was brought into being for these purposes. It met July 21-23, 1975, and again February 10-12, 1976, in Washington at the World Bank headquarters. A third meeting, held September 20-22, 1976, was hosted by the Asian Development Bank in Manila.

Organization and Operation

The organizational structure of CGFPI is patterned after the Consultative Group for International Agricultural Research (see chapter 7). It brings together donor countries and organizations with representative recipient countries to work out ways to increase the flow of resources to their agriculture and to use available resources more effectively.

The principal institutional members of the CGFPI are FAO, UNDP, and the World Bank, which provides the secretariat services for the Group. Also represented at CGFPI meetings are the regional development banks. Donor countries represented are Australia, Belgium, Canada, Denmark, France, Germany, Japan, the Netherlands, United Kingdom, and the United States. It was also expected that new donor governments, namely the principal oil exporting countries, would also participate, but they have not. Representatives from recipient countries were designated at the 1975 FAO Council on a regional basis: Brazil and Mexico for Latin America, Burma and Indonesia for Asia (Pakistan, India, and Bangladesh also participated in the second and third meetings of the CGFPI), Senegal and Sierra Leone for Africa, Sudan and Syria for the Middle East, and Turkey and Yugoslavia for Southern Europe. The regional conferences of FAO, meeting in 1976, confirmed the country selections initially made by the Council.

The chairman of the CGFPI has discretion to invite participation by individual countries or nongovernmental agencies when items on the agenda would be of special interest to them.

Participation by countries and international organizations is voluntary and does not obligate any of them to continue their attendance or to support proposals that come out of the CGFPI meetings. On this basis, Saudi Arabia and the United Arab Emirates were present at the first, but not at subsequent meetings.

The staff of the CGFPI is small, consisting of a chairman, four to six staff personnel, and an executive secretary. They are drawn from all parts of the world. A year after its establishment, there were no plans to expand the staff. The member international agencies helped provide data with which the secretariat staff produced papers needed by the delegates to discuss agenda items at each meeting.

Funding for CGFPI is provided by its three principal international organizations—the World Bank, FAO, and UNDP. The funding provides for the Secretariat, a limited number of consultants, and the usual requirements of office space and supporting services. The annual administrative budget of the CGFPI is small; after a year of operation, questions of additional financing for staff, contract studies, and possible in-country projects have been raised, but have not yet been answered.

Program of Work

The CGFPI is not an international organization with a large cadre of technical personnel, nor a financial agency disbursing funds for in-country projects. Rather, it serves as a forum in which critical issues may be addressed

26

by the countries and international bodies concerned, leading to possible actions on those issues. The semiannual meetings are informal and based on factual papers prepared specifically for the Group by its Secretariat.

The principal agenda items of the first two CGFPI meetings indicate the range of its concern and the views of the membership on priority issues the Group should consider. The first meeting (1) assessed investment needs related to the world food situation, (2) analyzed resource transfers for investment in food production in developing countries, (3) reviewed obstacles in donor and recipient countries to expanding resource flows and improving effective use of available resources, and (4) assessed investment needs for fertilizer production and distribution systems in developing countries.

The agenda for the second meeting included (1) a progress report on analysis of resource flows for agricultural development; (2) regional planning for fertilizer industry development, including distribution systems; (3) analysis of personnel needs and shortages affecting preparation and implementation of agricultural projects; and (4) assessment of investment needs for improved seed production and distribution in developing countries.

As indicated, a number of items discussed in the second meeting were updated reports and additional analyses of problems explored in the first meeting. Discussions on the selected issues have usually given rise to suggested courses of action, which are summarized at the meetings and in CGFPI reports on the meetings. In order to facilitate followup, the actions are listed for "recipient countries," "donor countries and institutions," and for the Secretariat of CGFPI.

At the third meeting of the CGFPI in September 1976, the principal agenda items dealt with the future of the Group and whether it could fulfill the objectives outlined for it in the World Food Conference resolution. The meeting had been preceded by discussions among the Group's principal sponsors—the IBRD, FAO, and UNDP—and they had prepared a report on the subject for delegates to the meeting. A conclusion reached by those attending the third meeting was that it was too early to determine the long-term value of CGFPI.

Assessment of Conference Impact and Followup Actions

The World Food Conference took place in the midst of a rapidly changing pattern of economic relationships between the industrialized and developing countries, precipitated in part by the successful deployment of economic power by the OPEC countries. Although other developing countries were hurt even more than the industrialized countries by the quantum increase in oil prices, many commended the oil cartel because it had demonstrated that a basic shift in the flow of the world's wealth was possible. Many developing countries have sought to use the UN system to achieve similar objectives. While some industrialized countries seemed ready to respond to the demands of the developing countries, most were not. But all were willing to use international forums to exchange views on the demands and to see if adjustments could be made. Hence, there has been considerable progress in establishing the new institutions called for in Conference resolutions, but accomplishments have been uneven.

While the 2 years that have elapsed since the Conference is a short time in which to gauge results, it is possible to identify where progress has been made and where difficulties and differences persist.

Increasing Food Production

Many of the specific proposals to increase food production embodied in Conference resolutions have been substantially realized. Higher national and international priorities have been given to increasing production. This is evidenced by a marked increase in the flow of financial resources—both bilateral and multilateral—for food and agricultural development in low-income countries. During 1975 and 1976, external resource flows reached almost $5 billion annually for food and agricultural projects, a target set by the Conference. This is almost double the dollar level in the year before the meeting. If the new International Fund for Agricultural Development becomes operational in 1977, the flow of funds will be substantially increased further. Resources for agricultural research have also increased in line with the Conference resolution. The Consultative Group for International Agricultural Research (CGIAR), at its meeting in October 1976, pledged almost $80 million for the coming year, up from $31 million contributed in 1974. FAO's Fertilizer Scheme continues its operation (though supplies are now more ample, and prices lower than in 1973-74). Through the FAO facility, over $100 million in subsidized or contributed fertilizers has been provided to needy developing countries.

Production of foodstuffs in developing countries, particularly the basic grains, were generally better in 1975 than in the previous 2 years, and the 1976 harvests have also been good. Even on a per capita basis, food production in developing countries recovered in 1975 and 1976 from depressed levels of 1972-74 to an index of 105 (1961-65=100), equal to the previous high achieved in 1970. Developing countries in Asia, as a group, recorded the largest gains. It must be noted, however, that improved production is probably attributable more to favorable weather than to increased external assistance which has just begun to enter the production system. Nevertheless, the increased flow of external and internal resources, if sustained, will make a difference in the years immediately ahead.

In addition to increasing the flow of resources, bilateral and multilateral aid agencies have directed their attention increasingly toward the problems of the poorer countries and the poorer sectors of the population. The international development banks have directed a larger proportion of their resources to reaching these groups by increasing support for integrated rural development projects.

Food Security

On the issue of greater food security, the evidence also seems positive. Policies and programs among the major food exporting countries suggest a willingness to maintain high production to meet both concessional and commercial requirements. Among most countries there is a new willingness to build and hold reserve stocks and to jointly consider ways in which stocks might, in the aggregate, provide security from serious shortfalls in food crops.

On several specific activities designed to improve food security, the responses to Conference proposals have been rather good. FAO has strengthened its Global Information and Early Warning System, and FAO's proposal on an International Undertaking on World Food Security received widespread acceptance. But the value of both efforts is uncertain, especially since the Soviet Union and the Peoples' Republic of China are not participating in the Undertaking or the Global Information System. Also in line with Conference proposals, FAO has established a new Committee on World Food Security, and the Intergovernmental Committee which provides policy guidance to the World Food Program has been enlarged in the number of governments represented and in the scope of its concern. These two committees are functioning.

However, for developing countries who consistently lack the foreign exchange to pay commercial prices for the foodstuffs they need to import, their security continues to depend on the goodwill of a few food exporting countries, most notably the United States and, to a lesser extent, Canada and the European Economic Community. Although the 20-year record of food assistance by these countries might offer adequate security, events of 1973 gave developing countries reason to want greater assurance. In 1973, the unexpected entry into the grain market by the Soviet Union with its large purchases led to sharply lower stocks of grains and sharply higher prices; some developing countries were almost squeezed out of commercial and concessional purchases. Also in 1973, oil exporting countries used their control over oil as a political weapon and the specter was raised that food could also be used for political purposes. Thus, although objective evidence indicates that stocks are being rebuilt and provisions for food aid are reasonably ample in the fall of 1976, international institutionalization has not proceeded as far as the developing countries wish. Some of the quantitative targets and multiyear commitments called for by the Conference have not been realized.

Increasing Trade Opportunities

The third principal issue dealt with by the Conference was that of enlarging export opportunities for food and agricultural commodities of developing countries. Developing countries most concerned on this issue tend to' see it as essential to overall development and to the establishment of a new international economic order. Progress on this front has been slow and both groups of countries—industrialized and developing—have been unhappy about the other's efforts.

Nevertheless, on trade matters, both the United States and the European Economic Community have made significant concessions to developing country exports and are agreed in principle on special treatment favoring developing countries in the Multilateral Trade Negotiations (MTN). In January 1976, the United States made operational a generalized system of preferences whereby hundreds of commodities originating in developing countries could be imported under more favorable terms. In April 1976, the

United States unveiled an offer to MTN participants of tariff cuts that the United States is prepared to make on 147 tropical product categories in which 1974 imports by the United States were almost $1 billion and most of these are from developing countries. But the United States has sought reciprocal concessions from other countries for making its tariff reductions. In 1975, the EEC announced a new trade and development agreement with some 46 developing countries (the Lomé Convention) designed to help increase exports of these countries to the European market.

But many developing countries with persistent balance of payments problems, and with levels of debt and export earnings which seem to stifle attempts at economic development, assert the need for a more general improvement in the terms of trade. During 1976, discussions on this fundamental issue were inconclusive at international forums such as UNCTAD IV at Nairobi (see pp. 119-120), and the Conference on International Economic Cooperation (CIEC) at Paris (see pp. 120-121). A general improvement in world trade prospects for agricultural commodities of interest to developed and developing countries might ease the process of accommodation. But the issues involved go beyond a transfer of earnings from more affluent to less affluent countries. A restructuring of the trading system is sought by developing countries—from one that emphasizes market forces and efficiency to one in which markets would be managed to give them greater equity. And that could mean fundamental changes in U.S. national economic policies.

3. FOOD AND AGRICULTURE ORGANIZATION

Background

The groundwork for establishing the Food and Agriculture Organization of the United Nations was laid at a 44-nation meeting held May 18-June 3, 1943. The first FAO Conference was held in Quebec, October 16-November 1, 1945; permanent headquarters were established in Rome in 1951. FAO's purpose is to raise the level of nutrition and to improve the production and distribution of food and agricultural products for all the peoples of the world. FAO is also concerned with improving the condition of rural populations and thus contributing toward higher standards of living and improved economies of member countries.

In serving the needs of its member nations, FAO has become the largest single organization providing agricultural technical assistance to developing countries. FAO focuses on all sectors of agriculture, including forestry, fisheries, crops, and livestock. It maintains working contacts with the other major international organizations concerned with agricultural development.

Membership in FAO has grown steadily since its founding; by the end of 1975, 136 nations had joined the organization. Most of the new members, particularly those of recent years, have been developing countries that made application to FAO as they acquired their independence. China resumed its place in FAO in 1973. The Soviet Union is not a member.

FAO funding comes from several sources: contributions from member countries, UNDP, the Freedom from Hunger Campaign (FFHC), and UNICEF. In addition, some FAO programs are financed by funds-in-trust arrangements with recipient countries, some by the international and regional banks under special agreement, and some under special programs financed by individual countries. Table 7 gives sources and amounts of funds for the years 1969 through 1975. As indicated in table 7, the regular program contributions (col. 11) are for FAO's basic program activities and these funds are from member country quota contributions. The other contributions are for specific purposes designated by the donor agency; hence, the table indicates both sources of FAO funds and how they are used.

FAO's program has evolved in line with the differing needs of its membership and the way these have been interpreted by successive Directors General. In its early years, a principal purpose of FAO was to collect and disseminate agricultural information that its member countries thought useful. Later, as UNDP took shape and FAO became a principal executing agency for its agricultural projects, and as FAO membership was increasingly comprised of developing countries, FAO became an important source of development assistance. This orientation has become more pronounced as a result of member views expressed in FAO's governing bodies during 1973-1975, and as interpreted by the Director General elected in November 1975.

31

Table 7--Sources of FAO funds and how they are used

Year	UNDP GCCC to UNDP/FAO projects	Government programs	Associate experts	Non-governmental programs	Other trust fund programs	WFP	World Bank and regional banks	Agency overhead costs	Total extra-budgetary activities	Regular program expenditures	Total FAO expenditures	Proportion regular program to FAO expenditures
	(1)	(2)	(3)	(4)	(5)	(6)	(7)	(8)	(9)	(10)	(11)	(12)	(13)
						Million dollars							
1969	58.1	2.6	1.9	3.0	1.4	2.0	0.8	1.2	8.7	79.1	32.0	111.7	29.6
1970	69.4	3.1	2.1	3.3	1.8	3.0	1.0	1.4	10.0	95.1	34.6	128.7	26.1
1971	85.7	2.7	3.4	3.6	1.8	2.6	1.1	1.9	10.9	113.7	37.9	151.7	25.1
1973	78.8	1.5	7.0	6.6	2.5	7.6	1.7	3.4	12.3	121.4	43.8	165.2	24.5
1974	78.6	2.3	8.8	8.3	3.0	16.4	2.0	3.7	12.8	135.9	49.3	195.2	26.5
1975*	90.0	2.0	11.0	10.4	3.4	55.4	2.3	4.4	15.5	194.3	59.8	254.1	26.6

*As of May 1975.

Explanatory notes:

Column 2. Government cash counterpart contribution administered by FAO.
  "   3. Bilateral programs administered by FAO.
  "   5. Contributions made under Freedom from Hunger Campaign and the Industry Cooperative Program.
  "   6. Foundations, international and voluntary agencies, and multidonor projects for dought relief operations in Sahelian Zone and Ethiopia, and for International Fertilizer Supply Scheme.
  "   7. The figures shown represent the cost charged to WFP for services provided by FAO.
  "   8. Contributions from the World Bank and regional banks for cooperative programs.
  "   9. FAO overhead costs paid for administration of UNDP and Trust Fund projects.

32

Organization and Operations

The supreme governing body of FAO is the Conference, which holds regular sessions biennially. Each member government may send one delegate to the Conference and each has one vote. Delegates are accompanied by alternates, associates, and advisers as determined by each government. The Conference acts on applications for membership in FAO, decides on the budget level and the scale of member contributions, and reviews and approves the Organization's program of work. The Conference also elects member countries to the Council, which meets between Conferences and serves as a second-level governing body. The United States has been a member of the Council since its establishment. At present 42 countries are members, an increase from the 34 that comprised the Council prior to 1973. Regional conferences are convened in each of the FAO regions every second year to discuss problems of the region and to provide guidance for the Conference and the FAO Secretariat.

Much of the substantive work discussed by the Council and the Conference is carried out by committees. There are standing committees dealing with program, finance, constitutional and legal issues, commodities, agriculture, forestry, and fisheries. The Conference and the Council also carry on their work through a number of *ad hoc* bodies such as the newly established Committee on World Food Security and the recently established Commission on Fertilizers. The Committee on Commodity Problems has a number of subgroups, known as intergovernmental groups, which provide forums for dealing with individual commodity matters. Other committees have been designated to work on *ad hoc* problems. The FAO Secretariat prepares substantive papers in connection with each committee meeting to provide a basis for more structured discussions in the committees and to have their conclusions serve as a guide to the FAO Secretariat's work.

FAO's scope of activities and funding levels have grown rapidly since its founding. While the regular program for the benefit of all members has increased substantially, the greatest increase has been in field activities for the benefit of developing countries. This reflects both the enlarged membership of FAO, mostly from among the less developed countries, and rising concern over the problems of providing enough food for the rapidly growing populations of these countries. Nearly four-fifths of the funds received by FAO from all sources were spent on field activities in 1975; this compares with about three-fourths in previous years.

FAO's organizational structure as of 1975 reflects its varied missions and activities (see fig. 4). Some recent changes introduced in FAO, but not reflected in the organization chart, should be noted:

- Creation of a Technical Cooperation Program Within FAO's Regular Program of Work and Budget. This new arm of FAO operations will provide (1) emergency assistance and rehabilitation for a country after disasters affecting its food and agricultural situation, (2) practical and vocational training activities, and (3) small-scale supplementary assistance that can be immediately useful to a country's food and agricultural situation.

33

FOOD AND AGRICULTURE ORGANIZATION, 1976

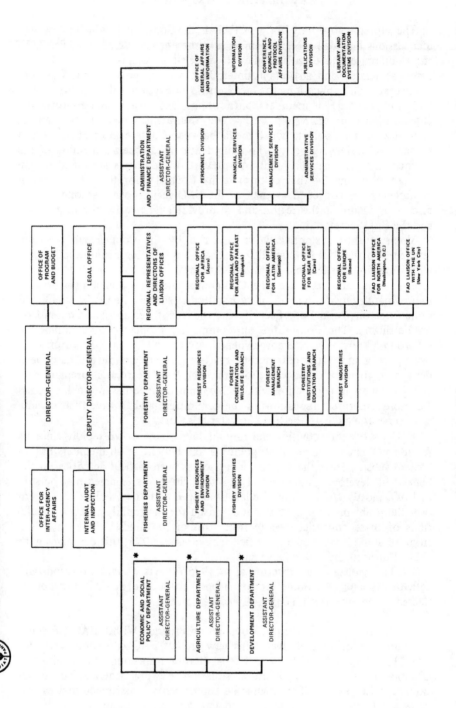

FOOD AND AGRICULTURE ORGANIZATION, 1976

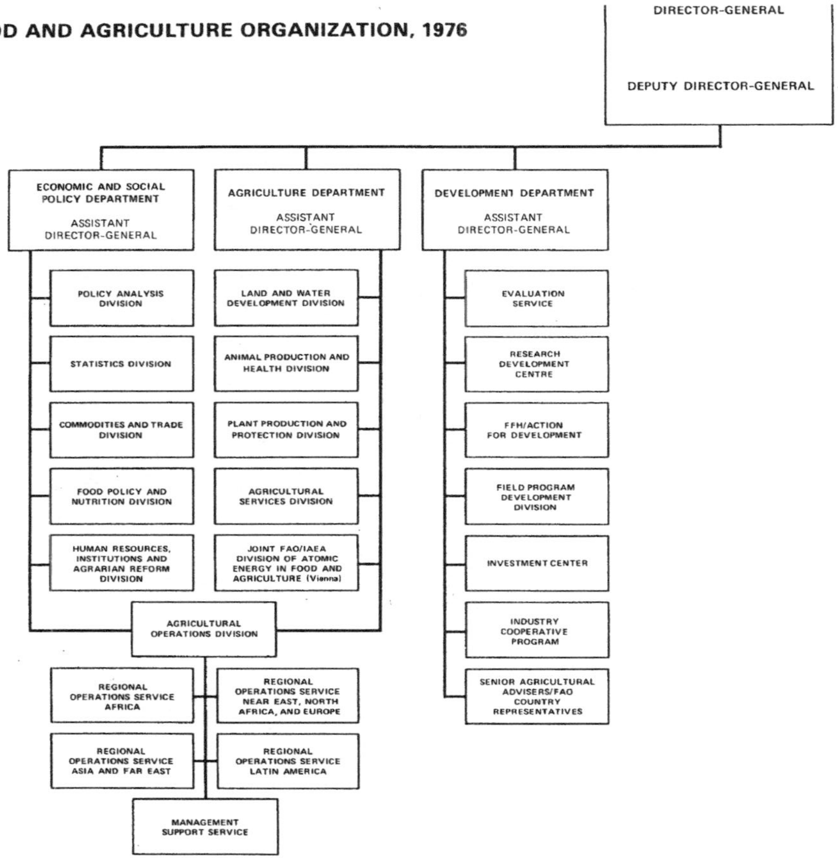

DIRECTOR-GENERAL

DEPUTY DIRECTOR-GENERAL

ECONOMIC AND SOCIAL POLICY DEPARTMENT
ASSISTANT DIRECTOR-GENERAL
- POLICY ANALYSIS DIVISION
- STATISTICS DIVISION
- COMMODITIES AND TRADE DIVISION
- FOOD POLICY AND NUTRITION DIVISION
- HUMAN RESOURCES, INSTITUTIONS AND AGRARIAN REFORM DIVISION

AGRICULTURE DEPARTMENT
ASSISTANT DIRECTOR-GENERAL
- LAND AND WATER DEVELOPMENT DIVISION
- ANIMAL PRODUCTION AND HEALTH DIVISION
- PLANT PRODUCTION AND PROTECTION DIVISION
- AGRICULTURAL SERVICES DIVISION
- JOINT FAO/IAEA DIVISION OF ATOMIC ENERGY IN FOOD AND AGRICULTURE (Vienna)

AGRICULTURAL OPERATIONS DIVISION
- REGIONAL OPERATIONS SERVICE AFRICA
- REGIONAL OPERATIONS SERVICE NEAR EAST, NORTH AFRICA, AND EUROPE
- REGIONAL OPERATIONS SERVICE ASIA AND FAR EAST
- REGIONAL OPERATIONS SERVICE LATIN AMERICA
- MANAGEMENT SUPPORT SERVICE

DEVELOPMENT DEPARTMENT
ASSISTANT DIRECTOR-GENERAL
- EVALUATION SERVICE
- RESEARCH DEVELOPMENT CENTRE
- F/H/ACTION FOR DEVELOPMENT
- FIELD PROGRAM DEVELOPMENT DIVISION
- INVESTMENT CENTER
- INDUSTRY COOPERATIVE PROGRAM
- SENIOR AGRICULTURAL ADVISERS/FAO COUNTRY REPRESENTATIVES

Figure 4-A

35

● Decentralization. FAO plans to decentralize more of its activities to have greater country level impact. FAO will also upgrade and strengthen its country representation and fund the costs of these representatives directly rather than share costs and direction with UNDP as they have in recent years.

● Investment. FAO plans to employ its technical staff more directly in the preinvestment process; it will provide assistance to countries and institutions in preparing projects for external investment in agriculture and agribusiness. It will seek ways of working with financial institutions and continue its cooperative work with the major international development banks.

● Increasing food production. Responding to the continuing crisis in food supplies for many developing countries, FAO is putting more emphasis on the basics of increasing yields, and less on social and economic analyses. It is also seeking ways to strengthen its support for agricultural research institutions in developing countries.

Within recent years, FAO has established an internal unit for evaluating field programs with a view to strengthening the formulation and implementation of UNDP and other field projects. In 1976, steps were taken to expand the evaluation activities to include FAO regular as well as field programs. The unit which carries on evaluations will be shifted from the Development Department to the Office of the Director General. This would give the evaluation staff a more appropriate location for reviewing all of FAO's work and reporting to the Director General and the governing bodies.

FAO activities may be divided into several broad categories or functions:

(1) Servicing FAO's governing bodies, that is, the Conference and Council, and the standing administrative and substantive committees; providing a forum for international discussions on world food and agricultural problems and for regional consideration of such problems.

(2) Collecting, analyzing, and disseminating a wide range of data on food, agriculture, and rural affairs of interest to its member countries; serving as the focal point within the UN system for such data, and for publication of relevant documents and periodicals; providing an early warning system and a focal point for international consultations on serious food situations.

(3) Providing technical assistance and training opportunities for developing countries in all aspects of food and agricultural development. Technical assistance and training is provided by executing UNDP country projects and projects financed from other sources, conducting seminars and workshops, helping formulate investment projects for international financial institutions, etc. Projects in the field are backstopped by FAO's technical personnel in the various substantive divisions of the organization.

Selected Areas of Work

The following are some principal areas of FAO activities; they indicate the kind of work done by FAO's substantive divisions, largely under regular program funding. This is not intended to cover all aspects of FAO's work.

Plant Production and Protection

FAO efforts to increase production of crops include a concern with high-yield technology, fertilizer and pesticide use, and advanced farming techniques. A major effort is given to transmitting high-yielding Mexican wheats into the Near East. On a national level, FAO advises governments on seed production and legislation. Attention is given to the production of industrial and protein-rich crops. In the area of crop protection, a major effort is now being given to evaluating potential dangers of pesticides. Studies are being made in cooperation with the World Health Organization on the residue effects of pesticides on humans. At the same time, research continues on insect resistance to common pesticides. Operational projects include assistance on improvement of forage and pasture crops, rangeland, fruit and vegetable production, training in modern horticultural techniques, and conservation of plant genetic resources. Headquarters backup support was provided to some 600 field specialists each year during the first half of the 1970's, and the number is expected to increase in the 1976-77 period.

During 1975, FAO began operations of its International Board for Plant Genetic Resources to conserve primitive plant varieties which possess qualities of great value to plant breeders. Symposiums on conservation of plant genetic resources were held in Bogor, Indonesia, and Leningrad, USSR. FAO sent out over 100,000 samples of seeds and other propogation material to regional nurseries, laboratories, and research centers throughout the world.

Some other examples of FAO activities aimed at increasing crop output include the following: There were new activities aimed at coconut improvement, e.g., FAO's working group on coconut production and processing met in Kingston, Jamaica to discuss, among other things, progress on hybrid production which could alter the economics of coconut cropping. A program was initiated to help developing countries learn how to use pesticides better and to protect the environment. Training courses were held in Bolivia and Panama on the safe and efficient use of agricultural pesticides, funded by the FAO/Israel cooperative program. A new FAO program on controlling crop pests gives promise of greatly reducing the need for chemical control. Tests carried out in FAO pilot projects show that new coffee strains resistant to coffee berry disease may be developed in a few years.

FAO support of agricultural research is the responsibility of the organization's Research Development Center. During 1975, the Center participated in some 300 projects in 80 countries. FAO continued to provide support for the Consultative Group on International Agricultural Research, particularly in servicing its Technical Advisory Committee (see chapter 7 on programs of the international research institutions).

Animal Production and Health

FAO supports operational programs, training and research activities, and dissemination of information to promote livestock production. Work is done on animal breeding and husbandry and the control of animal diseases. Animal breeding assistance usually takes the form of training programs, whereas the health program often involves large-scale efforts for vaccine production and distribution. FAO is called upon in animal disease emergencies, and often can provide vaccine on short notice. FAO assisted in combating a new outbreak of foot-and-mouth disease in Greece and nearby Turkish Thrace, and prevented further spread of the disease. It has supported university and middle-level courses in Afghanistan, Colombia, Dominican Republic, Ethiopia, Kenya, and Somalia. An FAO Regional Meat Training Center was established in Kenya with support from the governments of Kenya and Denmark; the center is host to the FAO/WHO training courses for meat inspectors.

FAO has begun a more intensive effort to seek means of controlling African trypanosomiasis, a parasitic disease borne by the tsetse fly which affects both animals and humans in a wide area of the continent suitable for livestock raising. A helicopter spraying campaign in Niger is being carried out as a pilot project by FAO with support from UNDP.

In 1970, FAO established an international dairy scheme to help accelerate development of dairy industries in developing countries. By 1975, some 17 donor countries and 48 other countries had joined the program of planning national dairy development programs. Five dairy training centers, located in Chile, Senegal, Uganda, Lebanon, and the Philippines, hold regional dairy training courses under a cooperative arrangement between FAO and Denmark. By 1975, FAO had conducted comprehensive dairy and meat development studies in 21 countries, and work to activate the conclusions of these studies was in various stages of negotiation with the countries and potential donor agencies.

FAO launched an international meat program patterned after the successful dairy effort. Its aims are to improve livestock production and expand supplies by improving animal health, animal slaughter, and processing. Some 43 projects have been identified under the program. The Swedish International Development Agency has agreed to assist FAO's meat program by establishing a trust fund of $895,000 to cover technical personnel and mission support for a 4-year period.

Fertilizer

After a year of acute fertilizer shortages and increased prices, which followed higher prices for oil, FAO established an International Fertilizer Supply Scheme in 1974. Although fertilizer supplies were more plentiful and prices declined in 1975, the continuing balance-of-payments difficulties of some developing countries led to a continuation of the scheme through 1977. It will likely mean over $100 million in concessional shipments of fertilizer to developing countries during the several years of its operation.

FAO has carried out a program of assisting developing countries in more effective and more widespread use of fertilizers. Under its fertilizer program, FAO helped organize some 3,500 fertilizer trials and 7,000 demonstrations to show how fertilizers may be used most efficiently. With financial assistance from the Norwegian Development Agency, FAO organized national seminars on mineral, organic, and other types of fertilizers in Ethiopia, Lesotho, Sierra Leone, and Cameroon. A UNDP/FAO project involving research institutes of

Bangladesh, India, Indonesia, Korea, Pakistan, Philippines, and Thailand will apply modern recycling technology to Asia's traditional use of organic materials as fertilizers.

Land and Water Resources

The problems of Africa's Sahel area, and the possibility that vast areas of rangelands in Africa and the Near East might degenerate into barren desert, gave new impetus to FAO work in soil and water management. FAO is joining with the UN Environment Program to assist 37 governments in the region in preserving their lands. In general, FAO provides technical assistance for pasture and crop improvement, appraisal of areas suitable for agricultural development, and development of national soil surveys and conservation activities. The forms of assistance include projects to locate water resources, preinvestment studies for irrigation projects, advice to governments on administration and legislation, mobilization of unemployed rural labor to improve water supplies, and applied research on fertilizer requirements for the new high-yielding crop varieties. In 1970, FAO cooperated in 10 large-scale UNDP-financed projects dealing with soil fertility and fertilizer use. By 1975, FAO was the executing agency for some 32 UNDP-financed projects on soil management. FAO became executing agency for a 6-year research project on land and water development in 20 countries of the Near East.

In addition to preparing publications on soil classification and methodology, FAO supplies scientific information resulting from its use of radioactive isotopes to trace underground water, and computer programing to determine optimal use of water resources. FAO helps conduct technical seminars and general policy conferences on various aspects of soil and water management. Major seminars on the subject were held in the Philippines in 1970, followed in 1972 by seminars in cooperation with the governments of Thailand and Korea. Also in 1972, the FAO Regional Conference for the Near East and the UN Conference on the Human Environment underscored the importance that land and water development should be accorded in FAO programs, and recommended establishment of regional centers for water management. Work on such centers is underway.

Fisheries

When Peruvian anchovy fishing fell off sharply in 1973, at a time of shortfalls in crops, the connection between fishing and world food supplies became more apparent to many, and the need for some international involvement in fishing matters was underscored. National pressures to exploit the resources of the seas, as evidenced in the international conferences on laws to govern national rights and harmonize national needs in such endeavors, have also had an impact on FAO's program in fisheries. FAO's regional bodies, such as the Indian Ocean Fishery Commission, are considering measures for a more rational harvesting of fish in the regional waters. Resources of inland fisheries are also subject to overexploitation as well as to risks of pollution. FAO, through its subsidiary fisheries committees, is studying ways in which countries can reduce these risks.

FAO carries out its program in fisheries with the advice of a Committee on Fisheries (COFI); it is open to all member countries of the organization and most countries participate. COFI reviews problems of fisheries and their possible solution by nations and intergovernmental bodies. FAO's Fisheries Department operates a fishing fleet of about 100 vessels, principally as a means of providing training. The major emphasis of the fisheries program is training and education. FAO estimates a 30-percent increase in productivity by participants in its training programs. A second area of assistance is the promotion of cooperation among nations and institutions interested in investment in the fishing industry. FAO also plays an active role in sponsoring international conferences and drafting international treaties on conservation of fishery resources. In 1973, at the invitation of the Canadian Government, FAO conducted an international conference on fishery management and development at Vancouver.

Each year FAO participates in almost 150 fishery development projects. Some 200 to 300 experts are included in these activities. UNDP-financed fishery projects in which FAO is the executing agency run from $10 to $15 million a year. Other fisheries projects are financed under bilateral programs and several are conducted in cooperation with UNICEF and UNIDO. FAO conducts international fishery surveys and feasibility studies to determine investment possibilities for public and private financial institutions and helps to focus their attention on such investment opportunities.

Food Policy and Nutrition

In recent years, FAO has put emphasis on helping countries investigate national food consumption levels and develop national nutritional services. During 1970-72, FAO was involved in 250 field projects which were wholly or in part concerned with "protein problems" in human nutrition. Considerable assistance is given to the establishment of food and nutrition units in ministries of agriculture. Other activities include education, promotion of protein foods, and group feeding. Home economics programs attempt to reach rural families and communities with information on the best use of food. Special care is taken to keep food innovations within the traditional dietary pattern of the developing countries. UNICEF finances many of the FAO nutritional projects, especially those involving improvements in nourishment of children and mothers. In 1972, the work on nutrition was given a broader policy orientation under FAO's Food Policy and Nutrition Division. In 1975, a Global Nutrition Surveillance Scheme was initiated. Linked with the FAO Food Information and Early Warning System, it will monitor nutritional conditions among the most deprived groups and will maintain a constant flow of information of the nature and location of food deficiencies. Also in 1975, FAO participated in a meeting of several international organizations responding to a World Food Conference recommendation for coordination of supplementary feeding programs for vulnerable groups.

Forestry

Interest is rising in forestry programs and projects from the viewpoint of resource use and employment. The number of FAO forestry projects financed by UNDP grew from 11 in 1966, with a budget of $14 million, to 62 in the 1972-73 period, with a budget of $50 million. In addition, FAO's Forestry Department administers some $8 million for projects carried out under bilateral programs with governments, trust funds, and the World Food Program (WFP). A principal aim of WFP forestry projects is to help in conservation and through reforestation and related work to create jobs for rural unemployed. FAO managed some 120 forestry projects financed by UNDP, WFP, and FAO's Freedom From Hunger Campaign during 1969-70.

The main emphasis in forestry is on education and training. In addition to advising many governments of Africa and Latin America on the operation of their own schools, FAO operated 27 forestry education and training projects devoted mainly to the production and distribution of forestry textbooks and the improvement of school curricula. Considerable attention is also paid to research on high-yielding varieties at both the theoretical and practical levels. Another area of activity involves surveys of forestry products and the means of marketing them. Recent years have seen increased emphasis on forestry development planning and on environmental conservation. FAO also has an active role in the conduct of technical seminars and forestry policy conferences. In 1972, FAO assisted the Argentine Government in conducting the Seventh World Forestry Congress in Buenos Aires. Over 2,000 foresters from 87 countries participated. The Congress adopted a declaration calling for greater development of forestry resources in low-income countries with due consideration to the environment and long-term social benefits. In 1975, FAO initiated a long-range program in Malaysia to integrate forestry development in the broader rural development plans of the Government. New legislation was drafted leading to the establishment of the Malaysian Timber Industry Board and the Sarawak Timber Industry Development Agency, with prospects for greatly expanded timber exports and foreign exchange earnings. FAO extended assistance to several countries on the administration of forest lands and forestry resources.

Training

In most projects funded by UNDP, an essential element is the training of local counterpart staff. This is not a simple matter. Often there is a lack of adequate counterpart staff, especially in such fields as economic planning, hydrology, animal production and health, forestry, and manpower planning. The problem is particularly acute in Africa. FAO feels that more effort is needed to improve counterpart capability and to assure continuity on projects for which nationals receive training.

Fellowships are provided by FAO to help train counterpart staff who are not trained directly in the field, and others for whom training would be beneficial. Traditionally, this has meant training in a more developed country. The United States, Western European countries, and the USSR provide much of the foreign training. Most of the FAO-sponsored nationals who come to the United States are programed by the U.S. Department of Agriculture. The Foreign Development Division of the Economic Research Service, USDA, conducts the training or arranges for other institutions to do it. Since 1951, FAO has administered over 10,000 fellowships, half of them in the last 5 years. Most are funded under the UNDP Special Fund fellowship program.

FAO regional training seminars and centers are becoming more problem-oriented and directly concerned with the needs of the participating countries. More advance preparation is also taking place to allow participants more interaction in the actual program. Approximately 50 such regional programs are operated each year. With growing competency among institutions in developing countries, FAO is increasingly directing training activities to these countries. In 1976, the Director General further reoriented training activities to increase their impact on the masses in rural areas; more emphasis will go to vocational training, and this is in line with the greater use of developing country institutions. There is relatively less emphasis on advanced training in educational institutions of the industrialized countries.

FAO training activities are aided through several bilateral cooperative agreements; for example, the Swedish International Development Agency supported training in Gabon, Mexico, and Ecuador on forestry development, and the Norwegian Development Agency also provided training assistance in forestry. Seminars on planning and analysis were held in Thailand, Egypt, and Kenya in collaboration with several bilateral donors. The Ford and Rockefeller Foundations collaborated on a workshop held in Tunis on the integration of wheat and livestock in rainfed areas.

Social and Economic Policy Initiatives

In recent years, FAO has sought to provide an overall policy framework for its country programs. The Indicative World Plan, which FAO completed in 1969, was designed as a worldwide analysis of the agricultural situation and projection to 1980. This work evolved into a Perspective Study of World Agricultural Development. In 1971 the FAO Conference agreed on this work as a continuing process, focusing on policy alternatives relevant for planning by governments. Country studies were aggregated to develop regional and worldwide analyses. Government requests for FAO assistance in agricultural development planning led to the establishment of several new teams specializing in various aspects of sector analysis. By the end of 1975, FAO had 22 such teams in the field compared with 14 in 1974.

International Agricultural Adjustment

FAO also initiated studies on international agricultural adjustment, a topic of interest to developed and developing countries, and an important item on the agenda of the 1973 Conference. Many developing countries had been concerned with the problem of earning more foreign exchange from their agricultural exports in order to sustain imports for general development purposes. And during the relatively good growing years of 1970-71, a number of developing countries with export potentials became concerned that they were unable to gain a larger share of the international market.

42

The FAO Secretariat provided a framework for looking at this problem under the heading of international agricultural adjustment. This framework noted that agricultural adjustments took place at three levels: (1) At the individual level, farmers or groups of farmers increase or decrease production in keeping with market conditions or leave their farms for jobs in the cities. (2) At the national level, governments have policies to promote increases or decreases in production, or off-farm migration. (3) At the international level, governments, working together, make adjustments in production and trade policy for their mutual benefit. FAO's work focused particularly on the need for and the nature of international forms of adjustment.

In connection with this work, FAO has published a number of case studies indicating how representative countries have made adjustments in their agriculture so they might better relate the rural sector to their overall development objectives or to market conditions. FAO also developed guidelines that developed and developing countries might follow as a basis for agricultural adjustments by FAO member nations. These guidelines were adopted by the FAO Conference in November 1975.

Underlying the FAO analyses is the proposition that developed countries might adjust their domestic agricultural programs and their imports so as to permit more exports by the developing countries. While such analysis served the interests of developing countries with agricultural export capabilities, the situation that overtook many developing countries in 1973-74 was a serious shortfall in food supplies and a balance-of-payments squeeze associated with higher oil prices and worldwide economic distress. Hence, FAO shifted priorities away from the longer term economic analyses and put more effort on the food supply problem of the countries most seriously affected by the world economic situation and their persistent inability to meet their food requirements.

International Undertaking on World Food Security

As part of FAO's effort to focus attention on the precarious state of world food supplies and stocks, it proposed that governments undertake concerted action to meet the problem. A proposal unveiled at the FAO Conference in November 1973 contained the following elements: (1) A statement that world food security is a common responsibility of all governments and that concerted action is needed to mitigate conditions of acute food shortages in the world; (2) an improved global early warning system; (3) intergovernmental consultations, with FAO providing the forum, in which necessary action might be agreed upon in the event of emergencies; (4) guidelines for national stock policies and for stock levels, and a recommendation that governments, where possible, should earmark stocks or funds for meeting international emergency requirements; (5) special assistance to developing countries for increasing their food production, improving their storage and stock policies, and meeting urgent food shortages by food aid, where necessary.

The FAO proposal was debated and supported in sessions of the World Food Conference, and governments were encouraged to signify their readiness to adhere to the principles and guidelines of the Undertaking. Following the

43

FAO Council meeting in the spring of 1975, the draft undertaking was sent to governments for their concurrence. At the time of the FAO Conference in November 1975, some 60 member governments representing over 90 percent of the world's grain exports had indicated they would take into account the guidelines of the undertaking in connection with their national food policies. On a recommendation of the World Food Conference, a Committee on World Food Security was established under FAO's Council to maintain continuing review of national and international actions pertaining to food security.

Other Programs

FAO provides advice and assistance on food processing, crop diversification, and mechanization. It is also concerned with farm management, agricultural engineering, and production economics. Focus is given to the earning and saving of foreign exchange through increased exports and import substitution. FAO compiles data on food outlook and conducts analyses for this purpose. It also produces information through economic analyses of completed projects, reporting this information in its several publications (which now include 10 annuals and 8 periodicals). The 1970 World Census of Agriculture was an FAO project and plans are underway for the 1980 Census. FAO deals with induced plant mutations, fertilization, and food contamination, and recent efforts have emphasized the study of pesticide contamination. It is also involved jointly with the International Atomic Energy Agency in research on the utilization of atomic energy in connection with food production.

FAO programs in cooperation with the World Bank, the World Health Organization, UNICEF, and private institutions are described in chapter 5.

4. UNITED NATIONS DEVELOPMENT PROGRAM

Background

UNDP, headquartered in New York, is the hub for technical assistance activities of the UN system. The present UNDP system was established in January 1966 as a result of the merger of the Expanded Program of Technical Assistance, set up in 1949, and the Special Fund, established in 1959. Currently, UNDP disburses over 85 percent of the funds expended by the UN system for technical assistance. UNDP responds to requests from member states for technical personnel and for help in developing project proposals that may attract investment capital. In implementing requests from member countries, UNDP usually asks one or more of the specialized agencies within the UN system to serve as executing agency. UNDP reimburses the agencies for the work they do. FAO serves as executing agency for most projects in food and agriculture initiated by UNDP. UNDP-financed projects are underway in some 147 countries and territories.

Projects of from 2 to 5 years' duration in such fields as agriculture, education, disease eradication, transportation, and resource exploration comprise the major part of the UNDP program. In addition, UNDP undertakes smaller projects in training and technical assistance to improve individual and institutional capability in developing countries. These types of projects are ordinarily executed for UNDP by other agencies of the UN system but some are carried out by staff of the UNDP itself.

Organization and Operations

UNDP policies are established by a Governing Council which meets twice each year, ordinarily at New York in January and at Geneva in June. The Council approves the program and administrative recommendations of the Administrator, and, since it is entrusted with the supervision of all UN technical cooperation activities, also reviews the technical assistance program financed from the regular UN budget. The Governing Council, which the 26th General Assembly enlarged from 37 to 48 members in a resolution adopted December 14, 1971, is composed of representatives of 21 developed countries and 27 developing countries. The United States has been a member of the Governing Council since the UNDP was established.

The UNDP has had several major changes in organization and operations since its establishment. During 1971, UNDP began putting into effect the various organizational and procedural reforms that had been called for by its Governing Council in June 1970. In part, these proposals followed the findings of the report, A Study of the Capacity of the United Nations Development System, prepared in 1969 under the direction of Sir Robert Jackson of Australia.

The UNDP headquarters was restructured; four regional bureaus were established with responsibility for the conduct of program operations. Authority for operational activities was decentralized to UNDP field offices, and resident representatives were given greater responsibility. The 25th General

Assembly of the UN designated UNDP resident representatives as leaders of the UN development system teams in their respective countries. Many of the resident representatives have representatives of FAO on their staffs as senior agricultural advisors.

In 1971, UNDP shifted from project to country programing procedures intended to help relate UNDP-financed assistance more closely to national development plans and priorities. Under the new country programing procedures, each country is assigned an indicative planning figure representing the amount of UNDP resources likely to be available to it over a 5-year planning period. Each recipient government, assisted by the UNDP field office staff and, where appropriate, by executing agency staff, then draws up a draft country program. This program outlines broadly the types of assistance the country wishes to have financed by UNDP over a period of time usually corresponding to its national development plan (which is usually for a 5-year period also). The draft country program is then appraised by UNDP and the executing agency prior to submission for endorsement by the UNDP Governing Council.

Once the country program is approved, project documents are prepared for each project. After appropriate appraisal the project documents are approved by the resident representatives in the case of small-scale projects costing less than $150,000, and by the administrator (or in some cases the Governing Council) for projects costing over $150,000.

The new country programing arrangements offer greater prospects for coordinating the assistance of the various UN system programs with those of the major bilateral and voluntary programs. This is in some cases being achieved by systematic consultations between governments, the UNDP resident representative, and the representatives of UN and other programs prior to the preparation of the draft country programs. In other cases, coordination is sought more informally or by *ad hoc* agreements.

In late 1972, the administrator's office was restructured to include two deputies—one for administration who has overall responsibility for UNDP administrative and financial procedures, and another for program matters.

A new financial system was also instituted in 1972. Abandoning its prior practice of requiring "full funding" of projects at their inception, UNDP began a practice of partial funding of projects at their beginning and trusting that subsequent contributions to UNDP from member nations would take care of later funding. This enabled UNDP to reduce its unexpended reserves to an operational reserve level of $150 million. But by 1976 this became one of the elements in a financial crises that beset the UNDP and which, in turn, was one of the factors that led to another major organizational and operational change in the agency.

In late 1975 it became evident that UNDP was facing a heavy financial deficit (in excess of $100 million). This was attributed to a number of factors, including inflation (it cost the agency $42,000 to send an expert abroad for a year, whereas $37,500 had been projected), high administrative costs, and most significantly, a shortfall in expected contributions by member countries. Some traditional donors found their legislative bodies distressed over actions in some UN agencies and reduced appropriations. Also, expected increases in donations from OPEC countries did not materialize.

In order to combat the deficit, UNDP undertook a number of strategies. It cut some administrative positions and overhead (such as limousines and hauffeurs) and travel costs have been reduced by 30 percent. Also, sharp utbacks were made and contracts canceled in field programs. The enforce-ent of mandatory retirement at age 60 and a freeze on hiring have effective- reduced personnel costs. Another strategy has been the increased use of trust funds" restricted to spending in the currency of the donating country. ence, an account built up in rubles might be spent for Soviet farm machine-y, if appropriate. In addition, member countries were encouraged to increase heir commitments. Sweden was the first to respond with a pledge of an dditional $5.6 million. The effect of such actions has been useful, and the verall UNDP structure has remained essentially intact. Figure 5 shows the P organization as of January 1976.

Program of Assistance

UNDP is supported largely through voluntary contributions of member countries of the UN. Budget projections are based on the amount each country has contributed previously, and upon pledges voluntarily agreed pon. In 1975, 129 member countries contributed a total of $406.5 million o the UNDP general resources. An additional $11.0 million was pledged by six countries for special aid to the least developed countries and other income of some $20 million was available. The U.S. contribution for 1975 was $90 million and for 1976, $100 million. Total pledges for 1976 are projected to be $450 million, excluding special contributions (49).

Recipient countries pay, in local currencies, an average of half the cost of UNDP-assisted projects. Such funds are used to pay costs of locally purchased supplies and services. The equivalent of $420 million was contributed by recipient countries in 1975; this compares with $357 million contributed in 1974.

While total contributions have been increasing, the U.S. share has declined. The U.S. contribution in 1975 was about 20 percent of the total; this com-pares with almost 32 percent contributed for 1972 and 29 percent for 1973. During the years 1972 to 1976, increased contributions have barely kept pace with rising costs of technical experts, but have not been enough to expand UNDP programs.

Several countries that have been recipients of UNDP aid have become net donors to the UNDP. Iran, Kuwait, the United Arab Emirates, Saudi Arabia, and Venezuela have all increased their contributions to the level where they at least equal the assistance they receive. The number of net donors is expec-ted to continue to increase. Over the last 10 years, developing country contri-butions have increased at the same rate as those of industrialized nations.

47

UNITED NATIONS DEVELOPMENT PROGRAM, 1976

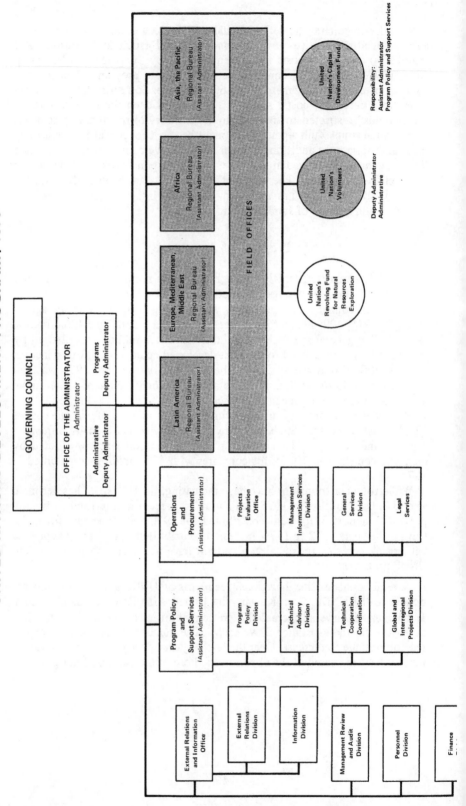

GOVERNING COUNCIL

OFFICE OF THE ADMINISTRATOR
Administrator

Administrative
Deputy Administrator

Programs
Deputy Administrator

FIELD OFFICES

Asia, the Pacific
Regional Bureau
(Assistant Administrator)

Africa
Regional Bureau
(Assistant Administrator)

Europe, Mediterranean,
Middle East
Regional Bureau
(Assistant Administrator)

Latin America
Regional Bureau
(Assistant Administrator)

United Nation's Capital
Development Fund

United Nation's
Volunteers

United Nation's
Revolving Fund
for Natural
Resources
Exploration

Responsibility:
Assistant Administrator
Program Policy and Support Services

Deputy Administrator
Administrative

Operations
and
Procurement
(Assistant Administrator)

Projects
Evaluation
Office

Management
Information Services
Division

General
Services
Division

Legal
Services

Program Policy
and
Support Services
(Assistant Administrator)

Program
Policy
Division

Technical
Advisory
Division

Technical
Cooperation
Coordination

Global and
Interregional
Projects Division

External Relations
and Information
Office

External
Relations
Division

Information
Division

Management Review
and Audit
Division

Personnel
Division

Finance

Working with nearly every government—and with 25 international gencies—the UNDP helps support some 8,000 development projects in Asia, frica, Latin America, the Middle East, and parts of Europe. The program operates in five areas:

● Surveying and assessing development assets (farms, forests, mineral deposits, fuel reserves, manufacturing and export potential, etc.),
● Stimulating capital investment to realize potential output and development,
● Providing vocational and professional training (including the establishment and equipment of local training facilities),
● Adapting and applying modern technologies to operate development projects in agriculture, health, education, industry, and other sectors, and
● Participating in the overall economic development planning of the other UN agencies—with emphasis on meeting the needs of the least developed countries and the poorest segments of their populations.

At the end of 1975, some 10,700 field experts were engaged on UNDP projects in 147 countries and territories, of whom some 1,300 were U.S. nationals. Of the project actions approved in 1975, $433 million were based on country programing 5-year projections and charged against the indicative planning figure budgets. The UNDP estimates that followup investment commitments from public and private sources to projects it initiated reached some $3.4 billion for the year.

Most of these UNDP projects are carried out by the specialized organizations of the UN system which serve as executing agencies. FAO is the principal executing agency in the field of world food problems and development of the agricultural sector in developing countries. In 1975, FAO was responsible for almost $120 million in UNDP-financed projects. Among other agencies that perform activities related to agriculture and rural development under UNDP auspices are the International Labor Organization (ILO), World Health Organization (WHO), World Meteorological Organization (WMO), United Nations Industrial Development Organization (UNIDO), and United Nations Conference on Trade and Development (UNCTAD).

While most UNDP projects are executed by these agencies, UNDP established a project execution division in 1973 to oversee projects that UNDP implements directly. During 1974 and 1975, the number of projects carried out directly by the UNDP increased sharply. Projects handled directly by UNDP are of a highly technical or multidisciplinary nature—including food processing, enzyme production, and off-shore food exploration.

Other Activities Administered by UNDP

The UNDP administrator is also responsible for four associated programs. These are the UN Volunteers, the UN Fund for Natural Resources, the Capital Development Fund, and the UN Fund for Population Activities.

49

UN Volunteers

On January 1, 1971, a corps of UN Volunteers (UNV)—an international peace corps—came into being. The 25th General Assembly in 1970 adopted a resolution (1) establishing as of January 1, 1971, an international group of volunteers to be designated collectively and individually as UN Volunteers; (2) requesting the Secretary General to designate the administrator of UNDP as administrator of the UN Volunteers and to appoint a coordinator within the framework of UNDP to promote and coordinate the recruitment, selection, training, and administrative management of the activities of the UN Volunteers; and (3) inviting member states, organizations, and individuals to "contribute to a special voluntary fund for the support of United Nations Volunteer activities."

The activities of the UNV continued to expand through 1976. Particular priority was given to getting volunteers on the ground in the least developed countries and to increasing the rate of recruitment from developing nations as a whole. As of August 1976, 285 volunteers of 47 nationalities were working in 48 developing countries, and 61 more volunteers were en route to their assignments. At the year's end, recruitment was underway for about 200 vacant posts.

The bulk of volunteer placements were with UNDP-assisted projects, including the United Nations Fund for Population Activities, the World Food Program, and UNICEF. These volunteers were serving in a broad spectrum of fields—as agriculturists, foresters, veterinarians, biologists, irrigation specialists, engineers, mechanics, economists, statisticians, architects, surveyors, teachers, teacher training specialists, nurses, and sociologists. The volunteers' contribution is particularly significant at the grass-roots level, where they work on extension activities in close association with the local population.

In keeping with longer term objectives, UNV has made the least developed countries major recipients of its assistance. By August 1976, 199 volunteers were assigned to 23 different least developed countries as compared with 89 at the beginning of the year in 17 of these countries. Requests indicate that larger programs can be foreseen in the future. An encouraging feature of the recruitment picture is the growing representation from developing countries. The proportion of total volunteers from developing countries grew to 47 percent by August 1976 and, on the basis of recent submissions, it is envisaged that in the near future close to 50 percent of all UN volunteers will be recruited from these countries.

Total contributions amounting to some $220,000 were made as of August 1976 to support UNV activities. Major government contributions were made by Denmark, Germany, Morocco, Belgium, Netherlands, and the United States (which contributed $75,000).

Fund for Natural Resources Exploration

Created by the General Assembly in 1975, this fund helps underwrite searches for economically useful mineral deposits. Repayment is required only when new mineral production actually results. In 1975, the Fund's apitalization stood at $5.4 million, and activities were underway in over 20 ountries. In addition to research for mineral resources, UNDP's technical ssistance in this sector spans almost the entire spectrum of natural resources levelopment, including policy, planning, and legislative measures; surveys and vestigations; prefeasibility and feasibility studies; training of national per onnel; transfer of modern technical know-how; improved research facilities; xploration; production; marketing; and trade negotiations. Activities have anged from new oil exploration in Indonesia to the search for suitable hydro lectric sites in Nepal.

he United Nations Capital Development Fund

Established in 1966, the UN Capital Development Fund (CDF) provides imited amounts of "seed financing" for such social infrastructures as low ost housing, water supply in drought areas, and rural schools and hospitals; nd for such grass roots productive facilities as agricultural workshops, ottage industry centers, cooperatives, and credit unions. The least developed ountries receive assistance on a grant basis. By mid-1975, 58 countries had ontributed a total of $17.9 million to the CDF's resources; $15 million of his was committed to projects, virtually all of which were concentrated in he rural areas. Agricultural production accounted for 62 percent of these ommitments, more than one-half of which were allocated to drought related activities. Small-scale agro-industry capital projects received 8 percent of commitments and rural schools and health centers 15 percent, while 20 per cent of CDF projects were allocated for credit purposes.

UN Fund for Population Activities

In operation since 1969, the UN Fund for Population Activities supports the efforts of developing nations to formulate and carry out sound popula tion policies. Specific activities include the collection of accurate data on population patterns and trends, assistance for voluntary family planning, motivational and educational campaigns, the provision of contraceptive supplies, the education of women in postnatal infant care, and biomedical research. The Fund's steadily expanding work during 1975 involved some 1,200 projects in more than 90 countries at a total cost of about $80 million.

5. COOPERATIVE AGRICULTURAL DEVELOPMENT PROGRAMS

Organizations of the UN family and others cooperate in many programs that further their respective efforts to assist the development of agriculture in low-income countries. This is an essential element of multilateral assistance because the development process is complex, and changed conditions do not necessarily fit into the prescribed areas of responsibility of any one international organization. If multilateral assistance is to be responsive to changing world requirements, collaborative efforts must evolve among existing organizations or new agencies will be called for. In this section, some of the cooperative efforts between international organizations concerned with food and agricultural development are described briefly. The cooperative support of international argicultural research is discussed in chapter 7.

The FAO/UN World Food Program

The World Food Program (WFP) owes its origin to the world agricultural imbalance in which some countries produce too much for their own needs and world markets, while others neither grow enough nor earn enough to purchase their food needs in commercial markets. Various proposals for international action to overcome the problems of commodity surpluses and food deficiences were discussed following World War II. In 1954, the United States initiated a large bilateral food aid program (widely known as the P.L. 480 or Food for Peace program) which gave further impetus to these discussions. In 1960, the UN General Assembly passed a resolution which requested FAO to study possible arrangements, including multilateral ones, for mobilizing and distributing available surplus foods. FAO prepared such a study, calling for a multilateral program with contributions in commodities and cash for a 3-year period. The program proposal was approved by parallel resolutions passed by the FAO Conference and the UN Assembly in 1961, and the World Food Program came into operation on January 1, 1963.

The life of WFP was subsequently extended for additional 3-year periods and then indefinitely. Pledging targets were set, and largely met, rising from the first $100 million to $275 million for 1966-68, $300 million for 1971-72, and $750 million for 1977-78. The U.S. share, originally set at not more than 50 percent of the total program funding, was reduced to 40 percent as more donor countries participated. However, for 1977-78, the U.S. pledge is $188 million, or about 25 percent of the target of $750 million. Pledging conferences are held every 2 years. Contributions to the WFP are made in cash or in commodities or transportation of commodities on a voluntary basis by donor countries.

The major objective of the program is to supply food for projects promoting social and economic development in recipient countries. Four types of projects are aided: (1) human resources development such as child feeding and school lunch programs; (2) infrastructure development—such as irrigation and road projects—in which part of the workers' earnings are paid in food; (3) production development projects such as the supply of feed grain to support livestock and poultry industries; and (4) resettlement programs to help displaced groups make a new start on land made available to them (until their first crops are harvested).

Feeding programs for children and related human resource development projects constitute the highest priority and the largest element of WFP activities. Typical of these projects are the following. In Colombia, the program has committed more than $43 million over 5 years for nutrition education and supplementary feeding of groups most vulnerable to diet deficiencies, such as the very young, the aged, and pregnant women. In Brazil's Sao Francisco Valley, free lunches were given to children to improve nutrition and promote school attendance. In Lesotho and Botswana, practically the entire school population has been receiving WFP assistance.

Aid for infrastructure improvement projects constitutes a second large element in the program. Roads have been built in many countries with WFP food assistance; workers (often locally unemployed labor) receive a portion of their salaries in the form of food distributed through the WFP. Housing, wells, and irrigation works are other types of projects in which food assistance has been an important component. Projects in the "directly productive" category include aid provided to India for development of the dairy industry and for marketing milk; dried skim milk is used to help increase milk supplies and hold down prices, thereby broadening the market for milk. Settling people on new land is a difficult process, and WFP has furthered this effort in a number of countries. In the Sudan, 115,000 were resettled, including 45,000 transferred from the area of the Aswan Dam in Egypt and 70,000 nomads; in Malaysia, more than 147,000 people were aided in resettlement projects associated with new rubber- and palm-growing operations. The WFP was one of the international agencies providing assistance to refugees from the drought in Sahelian Africa and Ethiopia.

WFP also assists in supplying food during emergencies. In recent years, thousands of victims of earthquakes, typhoons, and local wars have been helped. Three successive typhoons hit the Philippines in late November 1970, and WFP supplied nearly $2.4 million in food aid; two drought operations in India cost $7.4 million and $2.7 million in two successive years (18). In 1975, a drought-stricken area of Pakistan was assisted by food aid with a value of $1.5 million. In the same year, WFP aided flood victims in Honduras at a cost of $1.0 million.[1]

At the Seventh Special Session of the UN General Assembly, it was recommended that the WFP capacity to deal with emergency food needs to be strengthened by having donor governments provide it with cash and commodities to establish an emergency reserve of not less than 500,000 tons of food grains. Also, ongoing discussions in several international forums on questions of food security have raised questions about possible changes in WFP programs. In remarks by the WFP Executive Director and by FAO's Director General at the 1975 session of the WFP Intergovernmental Committee, it was suggested that WFP play a more important role in world food security measures.

[1]World Food Programme, Report of the 28th session of the UN/FAO Intergovernmental Committee, Sept.- Oct. 1975.

53

WFP is directed by an Intergovernmental Committee on Food Aid Policies and Programs. The terms of reference and membership of this governing body were broadened in line with a recommendation of the World Food Conference and an action subsequently taken by the FAO Conference and the UN General Assembly. The WFP governing body now consists of 30 member nations of the UN and FAO. Fifteen members are elected by the Economic and Social Council of the UN, and 15 by the FAO Council. Member nations are elected for 3-year terms and may be reelected.

The Executive Director for the WFP is appointed to a 5-year term by the UN Secretary General and the FAO Director General. The program is administered by a joint UN-FAO unit headquartered in Rome. The staff unit in Rome carries on the day-to-day operations of the program, including the review of applications for aid, the arrangement of shipments from donor countries where commodities are stored until required, and appraisal of results. The program's representative in recipient countries is the resident representative of the UNDP or the regional UN representative. WFP project advisers in the country are responsible to the UN officer. The WFP Executive Director submits progress reports to its Intergovernmental Committee on Food Aid Policies and Programs, which reports annually to the UN Economic and Social Council and to the FAO Council. They, in turn, report to the UN General Assembly and the FAO Conference, respectively.

The IBRD/FAO Cooperative Program

The World Bank-FAO Cooperative Program is designed to further agricultural progress in developing countries by combining the staff resources and experience of the two organizations for certain operations. The program, established in April 1964, seeks to expand opportunities for investment in agriculture and thus make a significant contribution to the development of less developed countries whose economies rely heavily on agriculture.

A major constraint on a rapid increase in IBRD and IDA lending for agriculture is a shortage of well-prepared high priority projects which the borrowing countries have the capacity to implement. The Cooperative Program is aimed primarily at reducing this constraint by assisting governments in identifying and preparing investment projects for IBRD or IDA financing. The final decision on whether a loan or credit is made remains with the World Bank, which also decides whether the financing will be on regular IBRD terms or concessional IDA terms.

The coordinating agency for all FAO investment servicing activities is the Investment Center in Rome. With the rapid expansion of field programs—especially under UNDP Special Fund financing—advice, studies, and investigations have become increasingly oriented toward investment. The information and expertise built up by FAO is valuable in the development of projects suitable for World Bank support. The growing gap between preinvestment work and investment financing may thus be bridged through the efforts of the two organizations.

FAO and the World Bank agreed that the most effective way for FAO to carry out its part of the Cooperative Program was to designate a team of staff members, drawn largely from the technical divisions of FAO, who would be employed full time on World Bank-oriented activities. These team members would acquire an intimate knowledge of the World Bank's approach and modes of operation, to enable them to advise countries in preparing projects for consideration by the World Bank. With this approach, the Cooperative Program benefits from FAO's expertise without disrupting its regular activities.

Close liaison is maintained with World Bank headquarters, and activities are jointly planned. Other arrangements include exchange of staff between the Cooperative Program team and the World Bank and joint seminars. Under the terms of the basic agreement, all missions undertaken by the Cooperative Program must be approved by the World Bank. Project identification and preparation missions are normally carried out under FAO responsibility, while all other missions are under World Bank responsibility.

The Cooperative Program aids governments in preparing projects, usually in two stages. The first, identification, consists of (1) a preliminary survey of the possible project to assess which activities should be included, what information is available, what has to be obtained to support a loan application, and the priority of the project and (2) discussions with the government on the organizational and administrative arrangements necessary to execute the project successfully. Identification missions, consisting of two or three people, usually spend about 2 weeks in the field.

The second stage consists of assisting governments in all aspects of project preparation. At this level, detailed critical analyses are required of the technical, economic, and financial data and the assumptions used in the project. The preparation mission helps the government assemble the detailed data needed by the World Bank to appraise the project. Some of the points to be covered are the scope and size of the project, the government's administrative proposals and their legal basis, economic policies affecting the project, the capability of the organization and management envisaged, the market outlets and prices for the product, the availability of local resources in manpower and finance, detailed costs and construction schedules, and implementation capacity of the government or project authority. The team composition must be tailored to the specific requirements of the project and usually involves specialists from a number of disciplines. Several missions may be necessary, particularly if there are serious gaps in the data.

Cooperative Program team members participate frequently in World Bank appraisal missions. Project appraisal involves a thorough study of the technical, economic, financial, commercial, managerial, and organizational aspects of a project with a view to deciding whether the World Bank will help to finance it and, if so, to what extent. This involves an evaluation of the data assembled during the identification and preparation phases, as well as formulation of the financing plan and implementation arrangements such as methods of procurement. Appraisal of a project clearly is the crucial stage in making a loan.

The terms of a loan often include provisions for technical assistance in the execution of the project and for complementary studies. Under the program, the World Bank may request FAO (as well as other institutions or individuals) to supply such assistance.

55

Since its inception, the program has worked on a total of nearly 200 projects in over 70 countries. The program has contributed to a greater diversification of the World Bank's investments in agriculture. Joint teams have worked on a wide range of projects, including livestock, irrigation, tree crops, credit institutions, cooperatives, forestry, and some integrated regional projects.

Rural development, intended mainly to benefit the poorest farmers, was the objective of more than one-third of the projects FAO presented to the World Bank. One rural development effort has been to help the Government of India draw up project proposals for intensive grain production on irrigated lands. In 1974, the first two such projects were initiated and, in 1975, a third project was funded at a total cost of almost $300 million for the three projects.

By the end of 1975, there were about 75 staff members for the IBRD/FAO cooperative program. In the period 1974-75, over 250 missions were carried out. About 35 of these were to prepare area and rural development projects and almost 20 were for land and irrigation projects.

Both the World Bank and FAO have continued to find their cooperative arrangements mutually useful and they have been renewed several times. The arrangements have helped the World Bank augment its own capability to develop financial projects in the agricultural sector and have given added relevancy to FAO's development activities. The experience of working with the World Bank on financial projects is one factor that has led FAO to consider using its own resources for identifying agricultural projects in developing countries for possible investment by development banks and other financial institutions.

Other Cooperative Programs

FAO/Industry Cooperative Program

In its effort to increase the flow of external investments, FAO promotes conditions for successful private as well as public investment in developing countries. This involves support of ongoing UNDP projects and the identification of potential projects for investment. Since 1965, FAO has been serving as a liaison between governments seeking development and industries interested in making agricultural investments. This work is financed by the industries themselves.

Some 80 multinational companies are cooperating on this program. Emphasis is on identifying projects and promoting government willingness to encourage private investment. Progress has been good in livestock, forestry, and food processing.

To provide an institutional base for this work, FAO established an investment center which helps bring managerial, marketing, and financial experts into projects to help ensure their success. For example, when a program mission conducts a survey of a particular commodity for potential investment, the government receives both an expert adviser and, at the same time, a potential investor. It is too early to evaluate the impact of the program, but it

s promoting investment in areas where investment by governments may not
e possible.

Through its investment center, FAO also facilitates the flow of resources
hrough private banking institutions as well as multinational corporations.
AO coordinates specific agricultural and agribusiness projects between these
rivate institutions in capital exporting countries and national development
anks in developing countries. Some 25 national development banks and
bout 20 commercial banks in developed countries are members of this work-
g arrangement. A recent example of the FAO/Bankers program was a plan
or the production of pulp, paper, and particle board from Egyptian sugar
ane prepared for the Arab African Bank.

AO/WHO Cooperation on Food Standards

FAO and WHO—through the Codex Alimentarius Commission—cooperate
n a food standards program concerned with developing international food
tandards, protecting health, and harmonizing national food legislation. Wide-
pread acceptance and observance of standards set by this commission facili-
ate the flow of food products in international trade to the benefit of both
eveloped and developing countries. By 1975, over 100 international food
tandards and codes of hygienic practice had been adopted by the Commis-
ion. They dealt with edible fats and oils, processed fruits and vegetables,
esticide residue tolerances, and labeling of prepackaged foods. Approxi-
ately 500 food additives have been examined toxicologically by an
AO/WHO joint expert committee. Another joint FAO/WHO committee of
overnment experts has drawn up a code of principles for milk and milk
)roducts, adopted thus far by 71 countries. By late 1975, 114 countries were
nembers of the Codex Alimentarius Commission. The Commission meets at
ibout 18-month intervals, but its work is carried forward by some 25 Codex
:ommittees that meet as working groups to formulate standards on which the
ull country membership may agree. FAO and WHO staff members concerned
vith food standards help developing countries formulate food legislation and
:arry out programs to enforce standards.

'AO/UNICEF Program

UNICEF helps children through its programs in nutrition and family and
:hild welfare. These activities are carried out in concert with a number of
)rganizations, including FAO. UNICEF also cooperates in WHO programs.
[he FAO/UNICEF program provides technical assistance to improve the
1ealth and nutrition of children and mothers. Areas covered by this program
nclude applied nutrition, milk conservation, high protein foods, home eco-
1omics, and education and training. FAO provides technical advice and assist-
1nce in project identification, appraisal, formulation, and implementation;
JNICEF furnishes material assistance in the form of supplies and equipment.
\n example of FAO/UNICEF cooperation is the construction of a plant to
)roduce high protein foods in Egypt. The program operates in over 90 devel-
)ping countries. Africa has the largest number of projects; Asia and the Far
East receive the largest allocation of funds.

Freedom from Hunger Campaign

Another cooperative FAO program is the Freedom from Hunger Campaign (FFHC). Organized in 1960 to educate the public about the world's hunger problems, FFHC has now assumed some operating programs as well. It works through national committees in 93 countries to communicate with the public in the developed countries and with farmers in the less developed countries. Its major operations program has been to increase fertilizer use in developing countries. To help this effort, the worldwide fertilizer industry contributes substantial amounts of cash and fertilizer. FAO carries out over 100 field projects financed through FFHC each year. Most of these are concerned with farmer training, rural communications, nutrition, education, and rural youth.

Increasingly, the FFHC efforts have been directed toward broadening support for FAO objectives and helping to channel extra budgetary resources for specific projects in line with FAO priorities. FFHC is particularly active in support of nongovernmental organizations, such as church organizations and voluntary groups, in their efforts to help the people of developing countries.

6. THE WORLD BANK GROUP

Background

The World Bank Group is comprised of three institutions. The International Bank for Reconstruction and Development—more widely known as he World Bank, or IBRD—is one. The others are the International Development Association (IDA) and the International Finance Corporation (IFC). They share the common purpose of providing and promoting a flow of capital nto productive projects and programs in their developing member countries. But they function in different ways.

● The IBRD makes long-term loans at conventional interest rates; most of the projects it finances are large scale.
● IDA lends for much the same kinds of projects, but deals with counties not able to bear fully the burden of conventional loans; its credits are very long term and free of interest except for a small service charge.
● For both IBRD and IDA, the criteria for making a loan or credit are he same. The project to be financed must make a significant contribution to he economy of the borrowing country, and there must be a reasonable certainty that the loan will be repaid. The loan or credit will normally help finance the foreign exchange costs of the project, although under certain circumstances IBRD/IDA funds may provide for local costs as well.
● The IFC is concerned principally with facilitating the flow of private capital for investment in private enterprise of developing member countries.

The general discussion in this chapter deals with operations of the IBRD nd IDA; references to the World Bank refer to both these agencies, except as pecifically noted, since IDA operations are simply a concessional loan adunct of the Bank. IFC activities are discussed in a separate section of the hapter because its operations are for private capital investments and hence re different from World Bank loans—whether on regular or concessional erms.

Organization and Operations

All of the constituent agencies of the World Bank Group operate under the ame board of governors and the same board of directors. The governors and xecutive directors on the two boards represent the member countries and ave a voting power roughly proportional to the total value of shares in BRD's capital stock to which the country has subscribed. As of June 30, 975, the United States had subscribed to 25.3 percent of the capital stock of BRD and held 22.6 percent of the voting power. The United Kingdom and ermany were the next largest subscribers, with 9.1 percent and 4.8 percent f the voting power respectively. Subscribed capital stood at $25.549 billion

59

of which 10 percent was paid in and the balance subject to call (*52*, 1975 p. 113).

Operations of IBRD are financed by funds from several sources. In addition to subscribed capital, IBRD obtains funds by borrowing on the world markets and by earnings which accrue from its operations and investments.

The IDA arm of the World Bank is financed on a somewhat different basis to permit it to make loans on concessional terms to developing countries. Funding for IDA is made up of (1) subscriptions and contributions from member countries, (2) transfers from IBRD's net income, and (3) income derived from IDA's investments and lending operations. An agreement concluded in September 1973 called for a fourth replenishment of IDA resources of approximately $4.5 billion. The U.S. share of this sum would be $1.5 billion, or 33 percent of the total replenishment. The U.S. share of the third replenishment was $960 million or 40 percent of the total.

In 1976, the World Bank was organized along the lines indicated by figure 6. The new structure establishes five regional offices, each headed by a Regional Vice President reporting to a Senior Vice President of Operations. During FY 1975, the Asia office was divided into the South Asia office and East Asia and Pacific office. Regionalization of operations provides closer integration of the area and project activities, and establishes even more firmly that the development of individual countries is the basis on which the Bank's program is built.

In addition to the six regional offices, the World Bank organization includes the position of Vice President, Projects Staff. This Vice President also reports to the Senior Vice President of Operations. He is responsible for providing functional guidance and assistance to the regional offices. His staff consists of selected experts who provide the support necessary to ensure uniform sectoral policies throughout the regional offices; certain specialists who cannot practically be allocated to any single region; and all personnel of the Population, Tourism, Urbanization, and Industrial Projects Departments—units too small to be decentralized at this time. This operating structure—the Senior Vice President of Operations, the regional offices, and the projects staff—replaced the former area and projects departments.

Each regional office has a chief staff economist, one or two country program directors, and a director for projects. The projects director is in turn responsible for four or five major sectors, such as agriculture, transportation, public utilities, and education. Within prescribed policy, each regional office has considerable operating autonomy, including responsibility for formulating the Bank's development assistance strategy in each of the countries in the region. The regional offices have the responsibility for planning and executing the Bank's lending and technical assistance programs in the individual member countries. The regional vice presidents are also charged with ensuring that necessary economic and sector survey work is carried out effectively and that identification and preparation work on projects is completed as planned. They are also responsible for project appraisal missions—from staffing to reporting—and they are responsible for negotiations and loan administration on all projects undertaken in their respective regions. For many projects, particularly those concerned with rural development, Bank loans will include monies under both IBRD regular terms and IDA concessional terms.

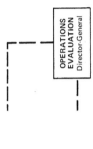

FOR RECONSTRUCTION AND DEVELOPMENT

MAY 1976

OPERATIONS
EVALUATION
Director-General

Figure 6

The regional streamlining of the organization has helped keep costs down as World Bank activity has increased. Between 1973 and 1976, the amount loaned by the Bank (on IBRD and IDA terms) increased 95 percent, while administrative costs increased only 69 percent. Personal services, consultants, and contractual services, the three areas of personal compensation, increased by 79 percent. Part of these economies result from larger loans, since much of the cost of project identification and preparation is independent of the size of the project. The number of loans granted by the World Bank increased by 45 percent between 1973 and 1976, and the average size of Bank loans increased from $28 to $35 million. In agricultural projects, the increase in loan size has been smaller, going from $27.8 to $29.7 million in the same pe   d.

Steps in Project Preparation

The World Bank follows a systematic procedure in preparing projects for IBRD and IDA lending. Individual projects are considered within the Bank's general assistance to a country and its overall development plans. The five basic steps in the granting of a loan by the World Bank are:

(1) Identification: The IBRD uses three tests to identify a project that may be suitable for Bank financing. First, does the sector in which the project falls have high priority in the country's overall development needs and will it have adequate local support? Second, is the project feasible in terms of cost and ultimate benefits? Third, is the project technically feasible and s ind? These questions are raised during the identification of any project. They may be relatively easy to answer where loans are "repeater loans" which arise from currently financed Bank projects. Much of the needed research has already been completed on this type. Projects may be suggested by the potential borrower or identified by Bank missions sent out to make economic or sector surveys of the countries. In the case of agriculture, FAO may participate as needed (see chapter 5 for discussion of the IBRD-FAO cooperative program.) Permanent missions, such as those stationed in Africa and Indonesia, may help identify projects in their areas. The question of whether a loan will be on regular IBRD terms or on concessional IDA terms, or a combination of both, will depend on the country's economic situation and on the kind of project being financed.

(2) Preparation: The formal burden of project preparation is with the borrower. The work is very detailed and involves development of all the specifications and various considerations needed to present the loan for appraisal. If the government is not able to carry out the study itself, it may hire a consulting firm or turn to other sources of aid. Sometimes this study is financed by the Bank with a grant or credit, but more often it will be done through the UNDP.

(3) Appraisal: After the preinvestment surveys are completed, the World Bank appraises the project to decide if a loan should be granted and on what terms. These studies are almost exclusively conducted by the Bank staff.

Typically, appraisal will involve a review of the following features of the project:

Technical features, such as the project design, site and material selections, cost estimates, and construction schedules,

Economic features, such as the project's role in the sector and in the country's economy as a whole, detailed benefit-cost analysis, and considerations of project timing,

Commercial features, such as the adequacy of marketing channels for output of the project and the arrangements used to procure materials and equipment for the project,

Financial features, concerning the availability of all resources required in addition to the loan for project implementation and, in cases of revenue earning enterprises, forecasts of the financial situation of the enterprise during operation of the project,

Managerial features, which have to do with the capacity of management personnel to direct the project and the possible need for advisers and management consultant services, and

Organizational features, concerning the administrative performance of the agency or enterprise carrying out the project, the need for organizational improvements, staff training, and the relation of the project entity to other agencies in the country.

(4) Negotiations: Negotiations with potential borrowers after the acceptance of a loan project through the appraisal process can involve many issues. The Bank not only negotiates the specific terms surrounding a project but, where necessary, other issues also. The Bank may, before lending, request commitments on various questions such as staffing, future support, and commercial matters not tied solely to the specific project.

(5) Supervision: After negotiations are complete and the project is approved by its Board of Executive Directors, the Bank has the obligation of monitoring the operation. Project reports are requested on a regular basis and are analyzed by the staff. Periodically, Bank staff will visit each project under construction or implementation. Usually, the Bank does not supply technical assistance at this stage, although in Africa, as mentioned before, the Bank and the government may agree on hiring project managers within the loan teams for countries that cannot meet the manpower requirements. While the project is being implemented, consideration may be given to "piggy-back" project elements that may be usefully added.

Technical Assistance and Project Preparation

There is a growing recognition of the importance of human resources in the effective deployment of capital assistance within developing countries. The World Bank often provides technical assistance and training in connection with its operations.

While the World Bank is primarily a lending institution, it does provide aid for preinvestment studies under special circumstances. As a member of the United Nations family, however, it cooperates with the UNDP, which has a major role in providing technical assistance for preinvestment studies. Since

63

1959, UNDP has asked the Bank to act as executing agency for more than 200 studies and other technical assistance projects, involving UNDP commitments of $140 million. In addition, the Bank joins with other UN organizations in technical assistance missions for identification of projects. For instance, during 1975, the World Bank Cooperative Program with FAO prepare about one-third of all agricultural projects financed by the Bank and carried out 143 missions in 50 countries. The World Bank Cooperative Program with UNESCO carried out 56 missions which led to the identification or preparation of 13 projects. Other joint programs involved about 26 technical assistance missions, of which 11 were for project identification or preparation.

Technical assistance is part of virtually every loan or credit, either in the identification, preparation, or implementation stages. In addition, financing may on occasion be provided for project preparation.[1]

The Bank recently set up a new facility to help governments in project preparation. This facility is used primarily to assist poor countries with limited capabilities for project preparation and initial implementation of projects, especially in the agricultural, education, population, and urban sectors. The funds advanced will normally be refinanced by incorporation in the project loan at the time it is made. During the first 6 months of its existence, the facility made commitments amounting to approximately $2.5 million.

The World Bank also provides technical assistance through its program of country economic missions, which is part of its continuing cooperation with the countries. These missions are intended to help in the process of designing strategies for the various sectors of the countries' economies. Teams may include UNDP representatives and technical personnel from specialized agencies, when appropriate. Missions will go annually to the largest developing countries, and every 2 or 3 years to others. This program is designed to facilitate financing of agricultural and other development projects.

Program and Operations Evaluation[2]

The World Bank has several evaluation mechanisms. For projects, evaluation consists of regular reporting by borrowers, periodic field visits by Bank staff, regular middle-management reviews of progress in solving implementation problems, a semiannual review by senior management of the status of the serious problem projects, and an annual general discussion of problems in project implementation. Experience gathered through supervision is also periodically assembled and analyzed by the Central Projects Staff which is responsible for reviewing, on a continuing basis, the Bank's functional policies and its programs in the sectors to which it lends.

---

[1]During FY 1976, 152 lending operations made provision for technical assistance for a total of about $218 million as compared with $160 million for 139 operations in FY 1975.

[2]This section draws heavily on "Operations Evaluation, World Bank Standards and Procedures," World Bank, 1976.

Program policy evaluation takes place through several offices. For example, beginning in 1975 the Development Policy Staff and the Central Projects Staff began evaluating the Bank's economic and sector work. Historically, budgets have been reviewed by the Programming and Budgeting Department. The *World Bank's organization is reviewed by the Organization Planning Department. The Auditing Department reviews accounting systems. Overall financial policies are evaluated by the Financial Staff. Recently the Research Committee has begun systematic evaluation of research projects. The Economic Development Institute has its courses evaluated by participants and participating countries. Individual departments do periodic reviews of their personnel, budget requirements, and projects.

The World Bank first established a unit for the express purpose of evaluating the "development-effectiveness" of its projects in September 1970. It was hoped that such a unit would help the Bank learn from its project experiences. The new unit was located in the Programming and Budgeting Department and was concerned with assessing the usefulness of individual projects and the impact of a group of related projects in particular countries.

Since 1970, program evaluation activities within the World Bank have increased in scope and acceptance as part of the Bank's operation. In April 1973, the President of the World Bank added to the work of what was then the Operations and Evaluation Division systematic project performance audits on all financed projects. The new procedure introduced evaluation at the close of project disbursement, to permit a review of the effectiveness and efficiency of Bank operations in order to identify possible lessons to be learned from the project.

As part of the World Bank's continuing efforts to improve its own system, several other changes have been made. In 1974, the Operations and Evaluation Division was upgraded to department level. In 1976, the post of Director General for Evaluation was established. Staff was provided from the old division; in addition to the departmental director and his chief evaluation officer, six senior evaluation officers direct the evaluation efforts in agriculture, utilities, transport, education and training, operational policy, and development financing institutions. Reports submitted from that office go to the Executive Directors of the World Bank as well as to its management. This established a degree of independence from line authority within the Bank without removing it so far from management that the evaluations do not feed into the system for improving project formulation and implementation.

The Operations Evaluation Department (OED) reports annually to the Executive Directors, but responsibility for assessing adequacy and efficiency is delegated to the Joint Audit Committee. The Joint Audit Committee reviews samples of OED reports, checking methodology and professionalism; it suggests policy issues to be recommended for consideration by the Board; it works out an annual budget; and it comments on OED's work in the annual report of the Audit Committee to the Executive Directors.

OED's project evaluation is increasingly based on project completion reports. These are done by the operation departments responsible for individual projects. They are not rigidly formal but rather try to assess the real issues. Questions are asked about costs, performance and economic returns, institutional development, and the efficiency of the Bank's work and the country's implementation of the project. The OED reviews all project completion reports and does an in-depth review of 10 to 20 percent of the projects. This constant information flow helps identify issues and procedures for which deeper evaluation and operational policy studies are needed.

Development Assistance in Agriculture

The World Bank's interest in agricultural development is almost as old as the Bank itself. The Bank made its first loan for this purpose in March 1948, less than 2 years after its creation. But agricultural development was not as important a sector to the World Bank in its early years as it is now. Substantial sums were lent for this purpose, particularly for farm machinery and irrigation projects, but the requirements of rebuilding the war torn world took precedence over development activities.

In the mid-1960's, the World Bank found it possible to support agricultural development on a much larger scale. From its beginning in the summer of 1946 until June 1963, about $650 million was lent specifically for agricultural projects. By June 1968, the total had risen to $1.3 billion. In other words, over the 5 years to mid-1968, the World Bank Group had lent about as much for agriculture as in all the previous 17 years. Its target for agricultural projects for the 1969-73 period was $2.4 billion and this was exceeded. In 1973 alone, agriculture loans totaled $938 million, more than double the 1972 figure of $436 million. Agricultural loans in 1974 amounted to $956 million and in 1975 they rose to almost $1.9 billion. The projected commitments for agriculture and rural development in the next 5 years are in excess of $9 billion. The Bank provides only about half the resources for the projects it supports, so the total investment involved is substantially greater (52, 1975, p. 16).

The World Bank's support for agriculture has been an increasing share of its total resources going for development in low-income countries. In 1962, agriculture represented 7.8 percent of total World Bank commitments. In 1971, they were 17 percent. In 1975, they reached 31.5 percent. A large part of the increases in agricultural loans is directed to rural development—efforts to improve conditions for 600 million people who have little or no land and who operate as subsistance farmers. The goal is to provide access to credit, higher yield inputs (fertilizer, seeds, pesticide, etc.), and education to help the rural poor make their farming more productive and remunerative.

The amounts lent for agriculture do not tell the whole story. Apart from the loans provided specifically for agricultural development, much of the money given for transportation, especially roads, has gone to projects intended in part to serve the needs of farming communities. The same is true of many loans given for electric power development. Indeed, a substantial proportion of the lending in other sectors, such as industry or education, has also helped agriculture.

Effective utilization of the increased investment being projected will require careful cooperative efforts by the World Bank and the countries involved, if traditional loan standards are to be maintained.

The World Bank's involvement in agriculture in the early years did not start with any preconceptions of what might be called "a grand design." Rather, it edged its way forward, selecting projects of high economic priority. The aim was to concentrate on the crucial bottlenecks in a country's agricultural economy that seemed particularly suitable for World Bank financing. The first agricultural loan was on regular IBRD terms and provided $2.5 million to Chile in 1948 for imports of agricultural machinery. Until the late 1950's, lending to purchase agricultural machinery was one of the Bank's chief functions. During this period there was a severe shortage of such machinery and of the hard currencies required to buy it from the main suppliers—the United States and other industrialized countries.

In the second phase, broadly covering the late 1950's and the early 1960's, a large share of the World Bank's agricultural lending went for irrigation and flood control projects. This emphasis has continued. For a variety of reasons, irrigation projects have proved particularly suitable for World Bank lending. They provide farmers with what is often their most important input—an assured or regulated supply of water. The capital cost of irrigation projects is usually high. Much of it is in foreign exchange. And that is where IBRD and its soft-loan affiliate, IDA, can be particularly helpful.

The World Bank program in agriculture has evolved in several important ways in recent years. First, investment is more diversified. While lending for irrigation is still the principal component, more loans and credit are going to land settlement, seed improvement, grain storage, livestock upgrading, forestry, fisheries, training, and extension work. Second, more support has been given to comprehensive sector analysis and overall agricultural development projects. Third, more loans have been made to investment credit institutions of member countries, strengthening their ability to extend credit as needed, particularly to smaller farmers seeking to utilize higher yield technology. The support is based on the realization that agricultural credit is vital for changes that touch most closely on the daily routine of the farmer. It can provide a large part of the resources required for the purchase of inputs such as fertilizer, as well as much of the capital required for investment on the farm itself. Agricultural credit is now the second largest category of the World Bank lending for agriculture, and its relative importance is growing.

A variety of institutional arrangements have been made for channeling credit to the farmer. In Mexico, credit has been routed through the central bank, which has then relent it through commercial banks. In the Philippines, the money has flowed to the farmer through small rural banks. In Tanzania, the agricultural credit agency has relied on the strength of local cooperatives to distribute credit. A common feature, however, is that the program of lending to credit institutions not only provides them with money, but provides them also with extensive technical assistance for improving their organization and operations.

Another important area of emphasis is livestock development. Its importance is viewed in terms of protein development and agricultural diversification. In recent years, the World Bank focused on livestock development where some feed could come from crop residues and silages, rather than from crops that compete for arable land. Great emphasis was also given during 1972-75 to increasing fertilizer production in the developing countries.

The World Bank is concerned with processing, storage, distribution, marketing, and other agribusiness activities, but this has not been a major area of emphasis. The World Bank Group has made loans for fisheries in Taiwan, Ecuador, Ghana, Tunisia, Indonesia, and Panama; storage and marketing in the Philippines, Pakistan, and India; and a fruit and vegetable export project in Turkey. It has supported other agro-industrial projects by loans through local credit institutions and development banks.

In recent years, the World Bank has given further emphasis to integrated small holder development. Work in this area is still evolving and depends on the applied economic research conducted by the Bank and the guidance provided by its Rural Development Department. Two kinds of strategies underlie World Bank investments in this area thus far: (1) Concentration on a specific cash crop of high potential as a focal point for general development in a region. Increasing output of this crop should help carry the economic burden of the several other elements in the rural project which are less susceptible to cost/benefit analyses. (2) Concentration on the overall development of a selected region, including all aspects of agricultural development—from the supply of farm production inputs and farm management practices to local marketing facilities to handle increases in farm output.

A policy paper on rural development published by the World Bank in 1974 characterized its work in this area as focusing on rural poverty and bringing the mass of these people into the mainstream of the country's economic development as both producers and consumers.

The trend in agricultural lending has been toward greater geographical diversification; the work now covers all parts of the world. In earlier years, most of the World Bank's agricultural lending was concentrated in a relatively small number of countries. Pakistan and India (including the Indus Basin Development Scheme) headed the list. The others included Colombia, Brazil, Iran, Malaysia, Mexico, Morocco, Peru, and Thailand. But the World Bank now has some kind of agricultural work in progress in 85 countries.

There were wide variations in the trends of agricultural loans between 1973 and 1975 for the five regions of the world, but in virtually all regions the level of commitments has risen. Western Africa increased loans eightfold during the period, from $50 to $323 million. South Asia increased loans from $93 to $400 million. East Asia and the Pacific increased borrowings by 70 percent; Europe, the Middle East, and North Africa by 88 percent; and Latin America by 64 percent.

Concentration in less developed countries has meant greater project preparation costs. In 1965, permanent regional missions were established in Nairobi and Abidjan, primarily to assist governments in East and West Africa to identify and prepare agricultural and transportation projects for IBRD and IDA loans. Elsewhere, notably in East Africa and Latin America, the World Bank has employed on contract a number of project managers who have helped governments implement projects the World Bank is financing on regular and concessional terms.

Training

The Economic Development Institute (EDI) was set up in 1955 by the World Bank to provide training services for member countries and to assist in broadening the perspective and enlarging the competence of senior officials of less developed countries who are concerned with the formulation and administration of policies, programs, and projects. The courses are designed to give the participants a broad perspective of the development process and an insight into particular country problems. The curriculum emphasizes practical considerations which will increase the effectiveness of these officials in discharging their responsibilities, particularly in connection with economic development projects. Courses are given in English, French, and Spanish and there have been 4,770 participants since 1955.

After reviewing EDI's activities in January 1974, the Bank's Executive Directors decided that there was a greater need for such training programs and that EDI's scope should be expanded. In order to multiply its effectiveness, they decided that more of the work should be done overseas, using existing institutions wherever and as far as possible, and that more efforts be directed at training trainers—teaching officials responsible for training in their own countries. In FY 1976, 11 courses were given in Washington, D.C., and 20 courses overseas; the number of participants has grown from 607 in 1973 to 429 for *the first half of 1976*. A small but growing number of courses are given in the languages of the host countries.

Another trend at EDI is the movement away from general courses to more specialized sectoral courses, such as rural development, urban projects, and education.

The EDI has a small full-time teaching staff. Personnel of the World Bank and the International Finance Corporation, including economists, engineers, lawyers, financial analysts, commodity experts, and country specialists, frequently conduct sessions when their special knowledge and experience are needed. Specialists from other international organizations, government agencies, universities, and private concerns are likewise invited to lead sessions related to their fields.

EDI offers project courses dealing with rural development, rural credit, and agro-industries. These courses are intended to familiarize senior officials with project analysis as a method of making the best use of capital funds for agricultural development. They also provide participants with information about the special characteristics of the agricultural sector, prospects for demand and supply of the main commodities, technological possibilities for expanding production, the role of marketing, price incentives and credit, and land tenure arrangements.

Among major elements covered in agricultural projects courses are: (1) analyses of rates of return on investments in agriculture; (2) analyses on a case-study basis of particular types of projects, such as irrigation, agricultural credit, processing, or marketing; (3) identification and preparation of projects appropriate for consideration by national officials and by international lending agencies; and (4) understanding the development process in agriculture and the place of agriculture within the national economy.

Participants are normally chosen from member developing countries. Generally they are attached to departments responsible for preparing or reviewing project analyses within ministries of agriculture, central planning groups, or other agencies concerned with rural development.

Agricultural Economics Research Activities

The World Bank's economic research activities have two principal aims: to establish a conceptual and factual basis for policy, and to provide general support to operations in a given sector.

Increased emphasis has been placed on the policy content of economics research; this is evidenced by designating the head of the Bank's economic work as Vice President for Development Policy, and establishing a policy planning and program review department. Moreover, each of the regional vice presidents has a chief economist as part of his immediate staff to relate economic analyses more directly to country programs and project appraisals.

Research support for the World Bank's activities in agriculture and rural development takes many forms: behavioral studies of the small farm sector, inquiries into specific aspects of rural change such as land reform and mechanization, and exploration of the potential for increasing food production and improving storage.

Investment decisions in agriculture are treated in research that utilizes regional programing models to determine what effect investment in improved production methods has on output, prices, and foreign trade. A model capable of interpreting these relationships for many individual crops, technologies, and cropping regions was developed. Stressing interdependence in production, the model's format allows for multiple crops and technologies (33 crops in all) to compete for the same land and production factors. In the study, Rural Development in Northest Brazil, a data set covering 8,000 farms has already proved valuable for several World Bank rural development projects. Current work entails quantitative analysis of the welfare position of small farmers, sharecroppers, squatters, and hired labor using extended versions of models like those developed in cooperation with the Government of Mexico. The extensions involved careful specification of land tenure relationships.

Other current projects take a retrospective look at World Bank activity in irrigation and rural development. A recently approved research project will assemble information on the management and organization of selected irrigation projects, and will later develop criteria for monitoring and evaluating irrigation projects, based partly on detailed study of a project in India.

Early research efforts on farm mechanization, now completed, analyzed the social and economic benefits of farm tractors in Pakistan. A related study, Agricultural Mechanization in India, deals with the impact of mechanization on farm productivity and employment in the states of Punjab and Gujarat.

Outside the policy aspect of its economic research program, the World Bank is endeavoring to expand its operations support. One effort is a program of monitoring project performance. A systematic data gathering and evaluation procedure has been built into several projects, such as the livestock activities in Mexico, Uganda, and Uruguay, and the Kadana irrigation scheme in India.

Additional studies concentrate on providing support to World Bank project work in specific areas. The Agriculture and Rural Development Department is designing a computer program that will process crop and farm budgets, as well as area and project budgets in model form, and produce cash flows using financial, economic, and shadow prices. Other research deals with the potential of crop and livestock insurance for increasing farm output and stabilizing farm income by reducing the adverse effects of crop losses; a review of the nonfarm rural economy; and the role of small industries in the productive activity of rural and urban areas.

Much agricultural economics research relevant to World Bank programs is underway throughout the world, and considerable attention is devoted within the Bank to reviewing and interpreting studies conducted elsewhere. This is an increasingly important source of new ideas for development policy. The content of the World Bank's own economics research program is determined by very specific policy needs or by the advantages of working with its own data. Nevertheless, many studies are conducted with the help of consultants or cooperating agencies in the developing countries.

International Finance Corporation

The International Finance Corporation (IFC) formally came into existence as an affiliate of the World Bank Group in July 1956, commenced operations shortly thereafter, and made its first loan in mid-1957. Establishment of IFC had been under discussion since the founding of the World Bank in 1947, but had been delayed out of a U.S. concern that it would compete with foreign private investment in the developing countries. As a result, its initial capitalization was small. Thirty-one countries became founding members of the IFC, with a total capital subscription of $78.4 million. By 1976, its membership had grown to 105 countries with total subscribed capital of $187 million and a surplus of an additional $78 million. For additional resources, IFC can borrow from the World Bank up to four times its unimpaired capital—a limit of $747 million as of June 30, 1976. A capital replenishment, which was proposed by the United States, would be paid in by member countries during the period 1978-82 and would raise subscribed capital by an additional $480 million.

Organization and Operations

Although a separately incorporated affiliate of the World Bank, IFC has the same Board of Governors and Board of Executive Directors as the World Bank because most of the same governments are shareholders in both organizations. The World Bank's President currently serves as Chairman of the IFC Board of Directors and as President of the Corporation. Both its staff and financial structure are separate and distinct from those of the World Bank.

IFC attempts to further economic development by promoting private investment in its developing member countries. It is unique among international development institutions in that it operates without a government guarantee on its loans and it purchases equity participations, that is, it may own stock in the enterprises it helps finance. IFC stimulates the flow of private capital into productive investments by bringing together investment opportunities, domestic and foreign private capital, and experienced management. IFC will make an investment only where sufficient private capital cannot be obtained by private enterprise on reasonable terms and where the investment will make a useful contribution to the development of the economy of the member country in which it is made. The investment must also have the prospect of being profitable.

The IFC does not finance government enterprises but is prepared to support "mixed" enterprises, i.e., joint ventures between a private enterprise and a government. Each case is examined in the light of such factors as the extent of government ownership and control, the nature of the enterprise, and the efficiency of its management.

The IFC also functions as a neutral intermediary between private enterprise and the governments of developing countries. Its basic interest is in economic development and its clients are companies and financial institutions in the private sector. It is concerned that public and private interests balance each other and the Corporation has earned a reputation for fairness.

It has become increasingly engaged in technical assistance in the area of private development investment banks and capital markets. Seven investments were made in this area in 1975. They included a mortgage and commercial bank in Bolivia and a financial intermediary in Korea. Technical assistance was provided to governments and private groups in 11 countries in 1976.

The presence of the IFC in an investment has been, in many cases, a determining factor in the decision of investors in capital exporting countries to participate in projects in developing countries. The Corporation has had a significant multiplier effect, generating more than $5 of private investment for every $1 of its own in the projects in which it has participated. Since its inception, the Corporation has been associated with about $7.8 billion of investments and has assisted in financing some 271 enterprises in 61 developing countries. IFC participates either in new enterprises or expansions. It has a current diverisified portfolio of 190 companies. Investment losses have been less than 1 percent of its total cumulative commitments.

IFC always acts as a minority partner and does not seek a significant role in management. Its contribution in all forms is generally less than 50 percent of an investment and it does not provide more than 25 percent of the equity and normally much less.

As a general rule, IFC works in conjunction with local partners. It may or may not be associated with a multinational firm. One of its long-term policies is to increase local ownership, and 70 percent of its holdings that it has sol have been to domestic investors. The FY 1976 projects represent a variety o ownership: 15 were locally owned, 5 were joint ventures of developing an developed countries, and 2 were businesses jointly owned by investors in tw different developing countries.

The IFC has set upper and lower limits on the size of its total participatio in individual companies. The upper limit currently is about $20 million. Thi is based on the rule of thumb that not more than 10 percent of its capital an reserves should be invested in any single enterprise. At the lower end, a million dollars is the usual limit because of the cost of loan processing. However, IFC does consider investments below that limit, especially in its least developed member countries.

Early in its history, from 1956 to 1960, small capitalization forced IFC participation to be small, averaging around $2 million per project. Its charter was not amended to allow equity investments until 1961. In 1965, it was permitted to borrow up to four times its unimpaired subscribed capital and surplus. This released all its share capital and some reserves for equity investments.

While World Bank loans under its regular terms are for 20 years at interest rates that are less than those of commercial banks, IFC loans are close to commercial terms of 7 to 12 years and interest is based on its own cost of funds and comparable loans in the commercial market.

In an examination of IFC's cumulative commitments by area, Latin America has the largest share with 39 percent, followed by Asia, 25 percent; Southern Europe, 22 percent; Africa, 10 percent; and the Middle East, 4 percent. IFC operations tended originally to gravitate toward middle income LDCs where industrialization is well under way and there is a business class with some wealth of its own to invest.

About 76 percent of IFC commitments have gone to manufacturing. Mining accounted for 8 percent of commitments. Development finance companies accounted for about 10 percent and the contribution was generally technical and managerial rather than financial.

Investment in Agriculture

Investment in food and food processing and fertilizers has been about 6.9 percent of IFC commitments, or $104.1 million, since 1957. Fertilizer projects accounted for $60.4 million, and food and food processing, $43.8 million. In 1976, 6.3 percent was invested for food and food processing and no investment was made for fertilizer. In 1975, about 4.5 percent was invested in food and food processing and in fertilizers.

The IFC has built a pipeline of agricultural projects by actively seeking investment opportunities in line with an increased emphasis on meeting world food needs and also in preparation for a probable increase in its subscribed capital base.

Recent Initiatives at the World Bank Group

The Third Window

The "Third Window," an intermediate lending facility, was established in the World Bank in December 1975, to lend at 4 percent less than the current IBRD rate. Thus it is a World Bank "window" midway between the regular IBRD terms and the IDA terms. This intermediate lending arrangement was designed to benefit lower income countries. And, although many very poor countries cannot afford to borrow even at this subsidized rate, IDA funds will be freed for their use as countries with stronger economies replace IDA loans with Third Window loans.

The new facility was authorized to lend $1 billion in addition to other World Bank operations. This meant that the World Bank would increase its lending over its projections by the amount of commitments through the Third Window. The Bank has had contributions of $129 million to subsidize interest, and total contributions are expected to be less than $150 million. This means that there are enough funds for interest subsidization on loans totaling about $600 million. All $600 million were probably committed by December 1976.

There was some concern that the Third Window would replace the purely concessionary loans of IDA. Therefore the United States, Germany, and Japan did not contribute to it. It is uncertain whether the Third Window will continue as an institution after its present funds are fully committed.

Development Committee

The Development Committee, formally called the Joint Ministerial Committee of the Boards of Governors of the World Bank and the International Monetary Fund (IMF) on the Transfer of Real Resources to Developing Countries, was established in October 1974, following approval of parallel resolutions by the Boards of Governors of the World Bank and the IMF. The Development Committee was established for an initial period of 2 years and in 1976 it was agreed to extend its activities for another 2-year period.

The Development Committee consists of 20 members, at the minister-of-finance level, appointed by the 20 countries or groups of countries that designate a member of the Board of Executive Directors of the World Bank or IMF. The Development Committee advises and reports to the Boards of Governors of both the World Bank and IMF on various aspects of the transfer of real resources to developing countries. The Development Committee also suggests instruments for alleviation of financial stresses, which can be adopted by the members or by the Bank and IMF. As an advisory body, the Development Committee does not make operational decisions regarding the instruments it suggests.

The Development Committee has made several important contributions in its first 2 years. It was instrumental in the creation of the Third Window lending facility by the World Bank. The Development Committee also helped bring about the Special Trust Fund of the IMF to provide balance of payments help. Neither of these ideas was new, but the high level consideration and political will generated by members of the Development Committee was considered critical in their implementation.

A third accomplishment of the Development Committee was a survey of the financial structure and needs of the regional development banks. Though less tangible a success than the Third Window and Special Trust Fund, it presents a change in direction of the Development Committee. Its first acts were in response to an urgent situation among developing countries. It is now taking a longer term view of the development process.

The Development Committee is also dealing with other longrun problems. One is how to improve the flow of official aid. Another concerns questions on financing of commodity agreements. This includes issues like buffer stocks and the compensatory financing facilities to help stabilize the export earnings of developing countries. The record thus far suggests that in a relatively short time, the Development Committee has become an effective voice for the developing countries in their quest for an increased flow of resources to them.

7. INTERNATIONAL AGRICULTURAL RESEARCH INSTITUTIONS[1]

Background

Agricultural research institutions have received much of the credit for the spectacular gains in production of wheat and rice referred to as the "Green Revolution." These gains, and the work of geneticists that made possible the new seed varieties, have received widespread recognition including the awarding of a Nobel Prize to Norman Borlaug for his work on wheat. The international agricultural research centers in Mexico and the Philippines, where the work in wheat and rice was done, have received their principal support from U.S. foundations. With wider recognition of the potential for increasing agricultural production in the developing world, support for an expanded program of international agricultural research became more widespread.

In his address to the World Bank's Board of Governors at its annual meeting in 1969, its President recommended that IBRD assume a greater role in promoting agricultural research institutions. He reported on discussions with representatives of the foundations and individual governments. Out of these discussions, and a subsequent conference in Bellagio in April 1969, grew the framework for a Consultative Group which would provide support for international agricultural research. The first meeting of the Group was held in the spring of 1971; IBRD assumed the role of secretariat.

The Consultative Group on International Agricultural Research

The Consultative Group on International Agricultural Research (CGIAR) is composed of IBRD, UNDP, and FAO; the Ford, Kellogg, and Rockefeller Foundations; the Inter-American Development Bank; and the International Development Research Center of Canada. Member countries represented at the first meeting were the United States, Canada, United Kingdom, Germany, Denmark, France, Netherlands, and Sweden. At the second and third meetings, other countries accepted membership: Australia, Japan, Norway, Switzerland, and Belgium. The Commission of the European Communities was given representation, as were the developing countries. Brazil and Argentina were designated for Latin America, Israel and Romania for Eastern and Southern Europe, Lebanon and Pakistan for the Near East, Morocco and Nigeria for Africa, and the Philippines and Thailand for Asia. FAO's Biennial Conferences in each of the regions designate two countries from the region to serve for the 2-year periods.

---

[1]Much of the material in this section is drawn from annual reports of the individual research centers, prepared, in part, for presentation to the Consultative Group on International Agricultural Research at its meetings in 1972, 1973, 1974, and 1975, from the report published by the Secretariat on the 1976 International Centers Week, August 1976.

The Group operates with the assistance of a Technical Advisory Committee (TAC) made up of 13 leading agricultural research personnel drawn equally from developed and developing countries, with FAO providing the secretariat. The TAC is responsible for reviewing programs and budgets of institutions that the Group may support. It makes recommendations on levels of funding by the Group for these institutions, and plans its own operations, suggesting a range of problems it might focus on and developing long range plans on international agricultural research needs.

At its second meeting in December 1971, the Consultative Group agreed to provide support for five agricultural research institutions. The five were:

International Maize and Wheat Improvement Center (CIMMYT), Mexico
International Rice Research Institute (IRRI), Philippines
International Center of Tropical Agriculture (CIAT), Colombia
International Potato Center (CIP), Peru
International Institute of Tropical Agriculture (IITA), Nigeria

The total financing recommended and agreed upon by the Group was approximately $15 million for 1972.

The international agricultural research centers meet each summer to review research programs and financial needs of these institutions. Each fall the Consultative Group meets to take up the question of support for the Centers and to consider other issues brought before it by the TAC. During the Centers' meeting in the summer of 1972, a sixth international research organization was added to the list supported by CGIAR, the International Crops Research Institute for Semi-Arid Tropics (ICRISAT), located in India.[2]

The third meeting of the Consultative Group took place in Washington, November 1-3, 1972, with IBRD serving as host. At this meeting, the Group made funding commitments in line with the programs and financial needs outlined during the earlier research centers meeting. Governments and organizations making up the group indicated their intention to make approximately $24 million available in 1973. The meeting considered the scope of operations to be supported within the Consultative Group framework and there was consensus that priority consideration would go for research on food crops. In this context, discussions were held on possible support for an animal disease laboratory for Africa and for linking African research stations to the work of ICRISAT. Questions of research on fibers and nonfood crops and the problems of synthetics, raised in a resolution by UNCTAD, were referred back to the TAC for further examination. There was consensus that the centers needed to be concerned with social and economic issues associated with the research, and with getting research results to those who ought to make use of them.

---

[2]Subsequently, the following research centers were added to the list receiving support from the CGIAR:
International Laboratory for Research on Animal Diseases (ILRAD)
International Livestock Center for Africa (ILCA)
International Center for Agricultural Research on Dry Areas (ICARDA)
Other research centers and agricultural research programs are receiving limited support from CGIAR.

77

During the Consultative Group meetings in 1974, it was agreed that support would be provided by several CGIAR donors for an autonomous institution to engage in socioeconomic studies. In line with this, a new International Food Policy Research Institute was created with initial support from several of the U.S. foundations and the Canadian International Development Agency. The Institute is located in Washington and reports to CGIAR, but is not formally linked to it. During the 1974 meeting, the Consultative Group and the centers focused greater attention on possibilities for an outreach program to bring their research findings closer to potential users.

At the meeting of the CGIAR in October 1975, the chairman noted that the Group would be embarking on several new ventures including the first quinquennial reviews of the scientific research programs of three centers by the TAC, and a review of the future growth and direction of the research network. Arrangements and a time schedule were agreed upon for both reviews.

The TAC then reported on its consideration of priorities for the research centers which included the following: (1) proposals for soybean research and research on other oilseed crops would be developed and reported to a following meeting of the CGIAR; (2) possibilities for research on a crop important to the balance-of-payments for many developing countries would also be studied; (3) possible factor-oriented research, e.g., fertilizers and pesticides, water management, and postharvest systems, would also be considered. The TAC also gave its views on the relationship between the international centers and national research institutions and expressed three appropriate relationships: (1) contributions by the international centers of materials   for testing, evaluation, and adaptation to national needs; (2) scientific services stemming from the international centers' core research programs, and (3) research aimed at identifying constraints to the adoption of the centers' improved materials or techniques.

The CGIAR meeting also discussed (1) action on a TAC recommendation that the Group provide $1.1 million to support the work at the International Center for Insect Physiology and Ecology (ICIPE), (2) progress on establishing an International Center for Agricultural Research in Dry Areas (ICARDA), to be located in the Middle East, (3) possible research on postharvest systems to reduce losses in food crops after harvesting (an expert study group on the subject would also look into institutional arrangements with the CGIAR), and (4) the International Fertilizer Development Center (IFDC), as an agency of interest to CGIAR but not requiring the Group's financial support.

Requests for financial support for the centers were put at $65.4 million. Pledges by donor countries, international organizations, and foundations reached a total of $64.4 million and there was some reduction in proposed budgets by the centers to bring them in line with available funding. Of the sum pledged, U.S. contributions were $16.1 million, or just under 25 percent, approximately the same proportion that the United States had provided in previous years. The Inter-American Development Bank contribution of $5 million represented a substantial increase over previous years; Canada's contribution of $5.56 million remained large; and for the first time, Saudi Arabia made a contribution, $1.0 million.

As the International Centers Week convened in the summer of 1976, onor countries and institutions again expressed support for the CGIAR ystem. They indicated that 1977 contributions would be about $80 million, hich would almost cover the aggregate requests made by the centers. Trends n contributions to the international research centers are indicated in table 8.

Table 8—International agricultural research activities funded by CGIAR

Established centers		$1,000		
IRRI	4,976	8,737	8,950	10,700
CIMMYT	6,072	7,316	11,218	12,500
IITA	6,658	8,771	10,758	10,200
CIAT	5,490	6,056	7,536	9,800
CIP	2,418	2,470	4,144	4,100
Subtotal	25,418	33,350	42,606	47,300
Newer centers				
ICRISAT	4,219	6,990	8,605	10,300
ILRAD	706	2,257	4,963	4,800
ILCA	303	1,905	5,724	8,100
ICARDA	–	350	3,300	5,500
Subtotal	5,228	11,502	22,592	28,600
Other programs				
WARDA	488	550	845	900
IBPGR	53	555	1,088	1,500[1]
CARIS	–	360	640	–
Subtotal	541	1,465	2,573	2,400
Total CGIAR	31,383	46,317[2]	67,771	78,300

[1] CGIAR Secretariat estimate.

[2] Preliminary; subject to revision upward.

A difference of opinion among the three sponsoring agencies, FAO, IBRD, and UNDP, on the appointment of a new chairman for the TAC was resolved by action of the Consultative Group.

Numerous significant achievements were cited by directors of the research centers. In Nigeria, the International Institute of Tropical Agriculture (IITA) demonstrated dramatic yield increases of cassava in farmers' fields using new varieties resistant to two major diseases of this crop in Africa. IITA also reported finding about 17 percent protein in one of its collections of yams, a starchy staple in local diets. In Kenya, the International Laboratory for Research on Animal Diseases (ILRAD) reported success in development of a method for growing the pathogen of a very serious cattle disease in Africa. This presages progress toward an effective vaccine against the disease.

Considerable stress was placed on reviews and evaluations; the CGIAR Review Committee was given broader responsibility for reviewing the future growth, direction, and management of the CGIAR network. Discussion was also directed to the need for a better way to determine cost/benefit relationships with respect to research supported by CGIAR.

Programs of the Research Centers

International Maize and Wheat Improvement Center (CIMMYT)

CIMMYT is an autonomous research institute established in Mexico in 1967. The institute is located near Chapingo, site of Mexico's National School of Agriculture and the National Agricultural Research and Extension Service. Research on wheat and corn had been going on for years at Chapingo, supported since 1943 by external grants and technical assistance, principally by the Rockefeller Foundation. Within Mexico, CIMMYT is active in six experiment stations, four under its direct operation and two controlled by Mexico's agricultural research institute. The 1972 operating budget of CIMMYT was approximately $5.7 million, exclusive of capital expenditures but including $1.6 million for special projects. In 1976, its budget was $11.2 million, almost entirely operating costs. The Center has an international Board of Directors, which includes Mexico's Minister of Agriculture and its Director of the National Institute of Agricultural Research.

Since its establishment, CIMMYT has concentrated its efforts on maize and wheat. Its objectives for the maize program are to (1) assist in the development of national and regional maize improvement programs, and supply technology for those programs that will especially help the farmers of developing countries; (2) increase the efficiency of maize yields in terms of production per hectare and costs per unit of production; and (3) improve nutritional quality of maize, particularly protein quantity and quality. CIMMYT operates the largest maize germ plasm bank in the world. The objectives of the wheat program are essentially the same as for maize. The program includes research on spring and winter bread wheats and durum, as well as barley and triticale (a cross between wheat and rye). CIMMYT does not maintain a world seed collection of wheat but turns to the U.S. Department of Agriculture for new varieties when it needs to augment its own working collection.

The institute has operated an important outreach program since 1960. In that year experimental lines of wheat were distributed for international nursery trials, and in 1971 similar trials were begun for maize. There are now over 800 separate trials in 78 countries. CIMMYT also conducts an extensive training program including short-term in-service training and work-study programs leading to graduate degrees conferred by universities in Mexico and other countries.

International Rice Research Institute (IRRI)

The year 1972 marked the end of a decade of intensive and successful efforts by IRRI to improve the productivity of rice cultivation. This institute is located in the Philippines under an agreement granting it autonomy of operation. The CGIAR allocated some $8.9 million to IRRI's operating budget for 1976.

The work of this institute includes plant breeding and trials under the three principal ecological conditions that characterize rice farming in Asia: (1) deep water or paddy rice in which the rice matures standing in water; (2) upland rice grown under controlled water conditions, either irrigation or controlled rainwater; and (3) upland rice grown without water control. The work of IRRI has concentrated on the second, since the high-yield rice strains respond most favorably when there is an adequate supply of water. The institute is working on disease-resistant varieties of rice and ways to combat disease such as blast, and is also developing varieties more resistant to drought. All these programs are aimed at making rice, the mainstay of millions in Asia and elsewhere, a more dependable crop, less subject to unexpected destructive forces. Another program at IRRI is aimed at improving cropping systems for rice grown in humid tropics; the hope is to increase productivity in these areas, which are found in many developing countries.

IRRI also conducts a training program which emphasizes programs for scientists at the senior level. Training includes work leading to a Ph.D. degree as well as postdoctoral studies. Special rice projects are conducted by IRRI in cooperation with research institutions in India, Sri Lanka, and Indonesia A project with Pakistan, which now produces surplus rice, was terminated in 1971. New cooperative projects were begun in 1972 with Vietnam and Egypt.

International Center of Tropical Agriculture (CIAT)

Although CIAT was formally established as a research center in 1967, its antecedents go back to a cooperative agriculture program established in 1950 by the Rockefeller Foundation with the Government of Colombia. CIAT is now completing building on its new site at Palmira, on the outskirts of Cali and adjacent to the Instituto Colombiano Agropecuario. The Faculty of Agriculture of the National University will also be associated with CIAT's program. The center's core operating budget for 1972 was approximately $2.9 million, exclusive of capital expenditures and funding for special projects. In 1976, the center was allocated about $7.4 million from the Consultative Group.

CIAT work is not concerned primarily with a single crop or enterprise but instead focuses on the identification and solution of tropical crop and livestock production and distribution problems, and on training people in a problem-solving research and educational environment. The two principal commodity efforts are in beef and cassavas, which together represent almost 50 percent of CIAT's operating budget. The Center works closely with national research organizations in Colombia to provide CIAT with access to tropical agricultural production problems and experiments in environments that differ from the headquarters location. The work in beef is concerned with overall systems of livestock production, including pasturage, range management, health, and the economics of a livestock industry under different Latin American conditions. A similar approach is taken in the program on ruminants. Crops research emphasizes cassavas and their overall

81

system of production, including the economic aspects of the industry. A limited program of research is being conducted on field beans and swine. Through its outreach program, CIAT is also involved in rice and corn research in cooperation with IRRI and CIMMYT.

CIAT training activities concentrate on providing learning experiences for selected professionals from Latin America and elsewhere. It conducts a 12-month course for crop production specialists and another on livestock production. The center's outreach program has thus far been limited to Colombian institutions. A new effort that CIAT is undertaking seeks means of integrating the production of several commodities into a single farming system to increase the economic efficiency of smaller farm units.

International Institute of Tropical Agriculture (IITA)

IITA was established in 1967 under agreement with the Nigerian Government. It has operated under a broad mandate to develop advanced technology which will enable farmers of the humid tropics to increase the quality and quantity of food production. The institute operates under its own Board of Trustees which includes representatives of the local government, donor governments, and research administrators of international stature. The institute had an operating budget of approximately $3.3 million in 1972, exclusive of capital expenditures. In 1976, its allocation from CGIAR was almost $10.0 million.

Among the institute's principal activities are (1) a farming systems program concerned with improving the cultural practices associated with farming in the humid lowland tropics; (2) a cereal improvement program that concentrates on two cereals, rice and maize, with the greatest potential for the African forest zones of lowland humid tropics (in cooperation with IRRI and CIMMYT); (3) a grain legume improvement program in which the research will be linked to the ecological conditions of the humid tropics; and (4) a root, tuber, and vegetable improvement program.

IITA maintains a library and documentation center which services its own needs and those of other African countries. The institute provides opportunity for training, but does not award degrees; it seeks rather to develop greater technical skill in the conduct of crop research and improved understanding of farming systems and farm management. IITA is also engaged in a number of special projects with other African countries and with support from sources outside CGIAR.

International Potato Center (CIP)

CIP was established as a research institution within the CGIAR framework in 1971. Facilities for the center are provided by the Government of Peru, which has granted it administrative and economic autonomy. The Center is governed by an international board of 10 members, including 2 from Peru and 3 nominated by the Consultative Group. A potato center was established because potatoes are widely grown in developing countries and if yields could be raised to levels comparable to those of European countries and the United States, potatoes would outrank cereal crops in the production of calories per acre. The Rockefeller Foundation International Potato Program, which had een operating more than a decade, was linked to the CIP in 1972. In 1976, e center was allocated some $4.0 million from CGIAR. The center is concerned with the development of different strains of otatoes, not only to increase output per acre but also to extend the range of cological areas in which potatoes may be grown efficiently. Most varieties re now grown in temperate climates and upland tropics, but it is anticipated hat they can also be grown successfully in lowland tropics and become a asic subsistence crop of these regions.

A principal research effort of CIP has been to build up a collection of otato varieties for trial and breeding purposes. At the same time, the center rovides a short-term training program and, in conjunction with other ducational institutions, courses of study leading to graduate degrees. Its utreach program includes the development of special projects between the enter and specific regions or countries.

nternational Laboratory for Research n Animal Diseases (ILRAD)

In 1973, an agreement was concluded with the Government of Kenya stablishing the International Laboratory for Research on Animal Diseases ILRAD) to be located in Nairobi. The primary and most urgent purpose of LRAD is to develop immunological procedures for preventing trypaosomiasis and East Coast fever, which are so destructive to cattle in a wide rea of Central Africa. Both diseases are blood-borne parasitic infections, the irst carried by the tsetse fly and the second by ticks. It has been estimated hat the territory in which these diseases frequently occur could support over ?00 million head of cattle.

Heretofore, attempts to control these two major hemoprotozoan nfections have met with limited success because of gaps in knowledge of the ;ausative organisms and how they operate. Recent advances in the mmunology and molecular biology of these organisms have increased the 1ope that the diseases can be eradicated from large areas of Africa. Although nany researchers are engaged in related research activities in many parts of he world, the solution to these problems will be greatly facilitated by the ?xistence of a coordinated, multidisciplinary, intensive program located in)ne of the endemic areas.

The laboratory in Nairobi conducts basic and applied research, tests results n the field, publishes and disseminates research findings, and establishes)rocedures for exchanges with other research groups to build on all relevant ?xperiences. In addition to its research related activities, ILRAD has an active)rogram of training and education. It holds seminars and workshops and)rovides on-the-job training of scientists and technicians. Although it is not a legree-granting institution, the laboratory works with universities in Africa ınd other parts of the world, and provides postdoctoral training in animal)arasitic diseases.

A basic operating principle of ILRAD is to provide scientific and training ıssistance to help develop and strengthen national institutions in Africa. It ⱱill also serve as a link between African research centers and the highly ;pecialized laboratories in developed countries.

The CGIAR allocation to ILRAD for 1976 is approximately $4.6 million—somewhat short of the $4.9 million originally requested. Contributions by the United States and the World Bank within the CGIAR framework amount to almost $3.0 million of the total.

International Livestock Center for Africa (ILCA)

In 1974, the Ethiopian Government and the World Bank, acting on behalf of the CGIAR, signed an agreement establishing ILCA at Addis Ababa. The purpose of the center is to assist national efforts to improve production and marketing systems for livestock in tropical Africa, so as to increase total output of livestock products and improve the quality of life for people in the region. The three main areas of activity are research, training, and the dissemination of information.

It is anticipated that the work of ILCA will directly contribute to increasing the numbers of livestock in Africa (estimated in 1974 at 130 million cattle, 100 million sheep, and 80 million goats) and the amount of meat and milk that might be obtained per head. Such increases would contribute significantly to improved nutrition for the people in the region and to their general economic development. This center will work toward opening up unused land for ranching, improving grazing lands and pastures, and generally upgrading herd management practices.

Although Africans engaged in producing meat by raising cattle and sheep have done considerable adapting to unfavorable climatic and other conditions, evidence mounts that much more is needed and can be done to improve output and lessen the rigors of current practices. Among the approaches ILCA is exploring are conservation practices to safeguard scarce water and grazing lands, application of research findings to improve animal health, and specific projects to test improved animal husbandry practices.

Two types of projects are sponsored by ILCA: "integrated projects" based on a multidisciplinary effort to accomplish particular objectives, and "associated projects" in which the Center will work with other African institutions to achieve joint objectives. Projects in the animal sciences will include genetics and physiology, nutrition, reproduction, and epidemiology. Environmental studies will be conducted on weather and soils, the ecology of rangelands, and pasture improvement. Some work in socioeconomic factors affecting livestock development will also be done, for example on marketing systems, social structure of pastoral societies, and relationships between producers and consumers.

The center will also be involved in training programs to increase the technical capacities of Africans concerned with livestock development. Seminars, conferences, and in-service training will be carried on under ILCA's auspices. The center will also offer consultative, documentary, and statistical services to national and international agencies involved in the improvement of animal production and distribution in Africa. Close contacts will be maintained with these agencies, particularly with the International Laboratory for Research on Animal Diseases.

The 1976 funds provided to ILCA through CGIAR amounted to $4.9 million. As in the case of ILRAD, a major portion of the funding through the

84

CGIAR is provided by the United States and the World Bank; together they make up about 50 percent of the 1976 funding.

International Crops Research Institute for the Semi-Arid Tropics (ICRISAT)

This research center is located in Hyderabad, India. It first began operations in 1973 and from the beginning had support from CGIAR. The mission of this center is to mobilize high-level scientific resources for a greater effort to improve the productivity of arid lands and the potential of dryland crops. The institute focuses on the small cultivator of humble means and the development of crops and farming practices that can increase yields without undue risk for the farmer.

ICRISAT places its emphasis on two cereals and two pulses, all major crops in these regions: sorghum, pearl millet, pigeon peas, and chickpeas. Also, ICRISAT seeks to develop systems of farming that will produce higher output and more dependable results year after year. Although the institute is new, its program of research builds on work done in India, the United States, and the Near East.

Elements of the ICRISAT program include the following:

Sorghum. New hybrid varieties are being sought with better genetic resistance to the most common disease affecting sorghum growth, resistance to mold in storage, higher protein content, and greater tolerance to cold weather and drought.

Pearl millet. While this is one of a large family of millets, it was selected for special effort by ICRISAT because of its widespread use as food in South Asia and Africa and its superior performance under adverse conditions. In addition to building on its proven hardiness, breeders are seeking greater yields and higher protein qualities.

Pigeon peas. This crop is grown widely and is particularly important as a food in India. Research is underway to reduce growing time so that double cropping may be possible. Also, short varieties are being sought that can be used in intercropping systems with grains to provide larger and more nutritious harvests for cultivators who are largely dependent on their own production for the kind of diets they have.

Chickpeas. This is another pulse of great importance in South Asia. The institute's goal is to combine in a single plant the traits that will give increased production, dependability, and high nutritional quality.

ICRISAT has made efforts to extend its research by exchanges with national research centers in the area and through a major UNDP project in sorghum and millet. Training is planned as an integral part of ICRISAT's activities, and in its first years arrangements were made for short- and long-term working visits by scholars and scientists in the region.

For 1976, ICRISAT was allocated some $8.16 million from CGIAR, the full amount of its request. Among the countries identifying their CGIAR contributions to the institute in India, the United States, Sweden, and the United Kingdom were major donors.

85

8. INTER-AMERICAN DEVELOPMENT BANK[1]

Background

The idea of a regional bank for Latin America is over 80 years old, having originated in 1889 at the First International Conference of American States. The Inter-American Development Bank (IDB) finally came into being in 1958 with the full support of the United States.

Although IDB is a completely independent organization, its establishment was negotiated within the framework of the Organization of American States (OAS). Negotiations were completed and an agreement was signed in December 1959. Nineteen Latin American countries and the United States became charter members. Several Caribbean countries joined later. Originally, membership was restricted to members of the OAS. In 1972, the Articles of Agreement were amended to admit Canada, bringing total Western Hemisphere membership to 25 countries. In 1975, a further amendment was approved to admit a group of nonregional countries as IDB members—seven European countries, Japan, and Israel. Other European countries are expected to join the IDB at a later date. (For an analysis of the several regional development banks, see (50).)

The IDB is one of the most important financial institutions in Latin America. Its purpose is "to contribute to the acceleration of the process of social and economic development of the member countries, individually and collectively." The IDB seeks to "stimulate public and private investment in development programs and projects, mobilize funds for development loans and related purposes, assist the member countries in orienting their programs for greatest effectiveness, and provide technical assistance as required." A large portion of IDB loans are devoted to agriculture. During 1960-75, agricultural loans totaled almost $2 billion, or over 22 percent of total lending. Other investments in the area of water supply, farm-to-market roads, rural electrification, and export financing have also had a substantial effect on the state of agriculture in the Latin American and Caribbean area.

Organization and Operations

Authority for IDB policy is vested in a Board of Governors representing the member countries. Voting on the Board is proportionate to the number of shares of stock held. The U.S. subscription is now approximately 35.7 percent of the total, Argentina and Brazil each have 12 percent, Mexico 8 percent, and Venezuela 6.4 percent. The combined nonregional members have 4.6 percent of the Bank's shares.

---

[1]Much of the material in this section is drawn from the IDB publication, Inter-American Development Bank, Structure, Resources, Operations, July 1972; the IDB publication, Fifteen Years of Activities, 1960-74, March 1975; and the Report by the Treasury Department to the President and the Congress on the Proposed Replenishment of Resources of the Inter-American Development Bank, September 1975.

The Board of Governors delegates power for Bank operations to the Board of Executive Directors. The Board of Directors has 11 members; 7 are elected by the Latin American members of the Board of Governors, 1 is appointed by Canada and 1 by the United States, and 2 by the group of nonregional members. The Executive Directors serve for 3-year terms and may be reappointed. The President of the Bank serves as Chairman of the Board of Executive Directors. The Executive Directors are headquartered with the IDB and function continuously, meeting as a Board of Directors as frequently as business requires. The President of the Bank is elected by the Board of Governors for a 5-year term and may be reappointed.

The principal operating divisions of the IDB are as follows: an Operations Department, which is divided by geographic regions; a Project Analysis Department, which includes a Division of Agricultural Development; a Department of Economic and Social Development which has two major divisions, one for economic and social studies and the second for technical cooperation and training; a Finance Department; an Administrative Department; and a Legal Department. The Executive Office of the President includes an Executive Vice President and a Controller. In 1976, a new Department for Programs and Planning was established, replacing the previous staff unit, the Office of Program Advisor.

The Inter-American Development Bank has, in recent years, developed procedures for reviewing internal operations and evaluating the impact of its programs. A Group of Controllers was established which reports to the Board of Directors on various aspects of the Bank's operations. The Board, in turn, requests the Bank management to study the Controllers' analyses and recommendations, commenting on and following the recommendations as appropriate. Also, there is a unit in the Office of the President and reporting to the Controller, which evaluates the effectiveness and impact of individual projects and programs that IDB undertakes.

Financial resources of the IDB include its ordinary capital (OC) and its Fund for Special Operations (FSO). Soon after operations began, the IDB also became administrator of the U.S.-contributed Social Progress Trust Fund. In 1975, Venezuela established a trust fund of $500 million under IDB administration. Within recent years, IDB has also administered funds made vailable by nonmenber countries outside the hemisphere.

Ordinary Capital Resources

The amount of ordinary capital authorized for subscription has been increased from time to time during the Bank's 16-year operating period to meet the rising volume of its activities. In 1970, the Board of Governors voted an increase of $2 billion, raising the total to $5.2 billion. Of the new money authorized, $400 million was paid in and the balance was callable capital—to be made available only if needed. The U.S. portion of the $2 billion was $823 million, of which $150 million was paid-in capital made in equal installments over a period of 3 years.

The latest increase agreed upon by the Board of Governors, in 1975, was for ordinary capital subscriptions of $4.45 billion[2] of which the U.S. share is to be $2.25 billion with $120 million paid in.

As of December 31, 1975, and prior to payments under the new replenishment plans, the Bank's ordinary capital resources subscribed to were $5.965 billion. Of this amount, $983 million had been paid in and $4.982 billion was callable. The callable portion of the subscriptions agreed to by the United States and other countries with strong currencies (such as Canada, Venezuela, and the new nonregional countries) provide IDB with the means for raising capital in private money markets to augment the amount of resources available for the Bank's lending program. Most of the money has been borrowed by selling bonds in the U.S. commercial market at relatively low interest rates since the bonds are guaranteed by the credit of the United States and other member governments.

The Bank has made agreements with nonmember countries for funding operations, principally by issuing bonds for sale in these countries. Among the other countries where IDB has made most of its borrowings are (as of December 31, 1975) Germany, $245 million; Japan, $145 million; Italy, $95 million; and Switzerland, $162 million. Through December 31, 1975, funds raised in these and other nations were in excess of $950 million. The admission of the nine nonregional member countries will further increase IDB possibilities for borrowing capital in world money markets.

Fund for Special Operations

The Fund for Special Operations (FSO) consists of contributions by member countries to permit IDB to finance projects under concessional terms. Operations and accounting of the FSO are kept separate from that of ordinary capital resources. Members' contributions to the fund are proportional to their participation in IDB's capital. The fund's authorized resources have been increased on several occasions to meet growing needs for concessional financing by Latin American members. Originally set at $150 million, the FSO was increased in 1964, 1967, and again in 1970, when the equivalent of $1.5 billion was approved by the Board of Governors, with the United States agreeing to contribute $1 billion which has been fully subscribed.

The 1975 proposal on replenishment of the FSO is for $1.045 billion with the U.S. share being $600 million payable in equal annual installments over the period FY 1977 through 1979. The new replenishment would mean a reduction of the U.S. proportion of FSO funds from 66 percent to 57 percent. Repayments of loans, interest, and other earnings from the fund are available for new operations.

Most of IDB's agricultural loans are financed from the FSO. Interest rates for FSO loans to the more developed countries such as Argentina, Brazil,

---

[2]This amount excludes the extraregional ordinary capital share which, with the admission of the nine new countries, amounts to $296.6 million.

exico, and Venezuela are 3 to 4 percent and such concessional terms are
vailable to these countries only for projects which have a predominately
ocial purpose, e.g., to further agricultural cooperatives. The interest rate for
ther countries is 2 percent for FSO loans except in the least developed
ountries where it is 1 percent during the grace period. A commitment fee of
ne-half of 1 percent per annum on the undisbursed portion of the loan is
harged in addition to interest. Under certain circumstances a service charge
f three-fourths of 1 percent is also charged. Starting in 1973, all FSO loans
re repayable in the currency lent which usually means in U.S. dollars or other
onvertible currencies. Loans have different grace periods and periods of
ortization, depending upon the level of development of the borrowing
)untries. These vary from a maximum grace period of 5 years and a
aximum amortization period of 25 years in the more developed countries,
o 10 years and 40 years, respectively, in the less developed countries.

The average loan from the FSO for the more developed countries covers
bout one-half of the project cost, while for the lesser developed group it may
each up to 90 percent of project costs; the remainder is made up by the
recipient country. This policy, promulgated in 1972, provides preferential
treatment to the region's economically less developed countries.

rust Funds

Another kind of resource available for IDB operations is funds
administered under trust arrangements with specific stipulations
covering the use of such funds. The Social Progress Trust Fund (SPTF) came
into being under an agreement between the United States and IDB in 1961.
This fund was augmented in 1964 bringing the total resources available to
$525 million. The SPTF was used to finance on concessional terms projects
to strengthen local institutions and thereby to encourage use of additional
Latin American funds for social improvements.

While the original SPTF is now fully disbursed, activities formerly financed
by it are now financed by resources of the FSO. Repayments of loans made
from the SPTF are used to purchase participations in FSO loans. Repayments
are also used to finance new loans and technical assistance on a grant or
reimbursable basis in particular fields, including agriculture. Many of the
grants derived from SPTF repayments and provided in 1975 went to sponsor
activities which could benefit the most impoverished groups of Latin
America.

During 1975, the IDB signed agreements with Venezuela to administer a
$500-million trust fund. This will provide resources for development of the
region's productive and exporting capacity. The IDB will use the Venezuelan
fund to finance projects concerned with use of nonrenewable natural
resources and hydroelectric resources, and for the promotion of agro-industry
including forestry. The fund will be used particularly in the relatively less
developed countries and those of intermediate economies. Loans from this
fund will be at interest rates equal to those prevailing for ordinary IDB
operations, with amortization over somewhat longer periods.

89

Assistance for Agricultural Development

IDB considers agriculture to be a most important sector in Latin American development; no sector received a larger amount of financial or technical assistance during the period 1961-75.

During 1961-75, the IDB provided almost $2.0 billion in loans to the agricultural sectors of Latin American member countries. Years of high lending in agriculture have tended to be followed by years of reduced programs, but the 16-year (1961-75) trend has been upward in absolute amounts and has remained high as a percentage of total IDB program lending (see table 9).

Table 9—Agricultural project loans as share of total loans, Inter-American Development Bank, 1961-76

Average:	Million dollars	Percent
1961-2	57.2	11.9
1963-4	70.2	22.0
1965-6	70.8	18.8
1967-8	110.0	23.6
1969-70	219.0	34.5
1971-2	112.0	15.3
1973	187.0	21.0
1974	228.0	21.0
1975	332.0	24.1
1976 (estimated)	450.0	29.0

Source: Internal IDB documents, especially Banco Inter-Americano de Desarrolo, Resumen de Prestamos, 1971, and Annual Report, 1975, issued May 1976.

Most of the agricultural projects are financed through the Fund for Special Operations and trust accounts; over $880 million came from these sources and $280 million from ordinary capital during the 11-year period, 1961-72; the proportions have remained the same in more recent years.

The largest single category of funding in the agricultural sector is for irrigation to improve and increase the acreage available for cropping. The emphasis is on irrigation dams and canals. Again, special attention is directed to the needs of the small farmer. Mexico, for example, has been the recipient of a number of IDB loans for small irrigation projects which will eventually provide water to about 3.6 million acres. The next largest category of loans has been for national agricultural credit facilities supported in part by IDB. Through these agencies, low-income farmers can obtain loans for machinery, seeds, fertilizer, and other inputs which can enable them to raise production from subsistence levels. The IDB provides extensive technical assistance to these credit institutions in the form of training and guidance. This reflects continued emphasis on providing credit facilities to small and medium-size farmers. It also demonstrates continued concern with strengthening the operation and administration of national credit institutions servicing them.

Commitments to infrastructure considered vital to increased production, such as rural electrification and transportation, are not included in agricultural sector fundings. Table 10 shows IDB agricultural lending for various subsectors during the period 1961-75.

Table 10—IDB agricultural lending by subsectors, 1961—75

Activity	Amount	Percent of total
	Millions dollars	*Percent*
Irrigation	$ 657.2	33.3
Agricultural credit	634.2	32.1
Integrated agricultural and/or rural development	206.9	10.5
Land settlement and agrarian reform	123.2	6.2
Livestock production	85.3	4.3
Animal health	78.7	4.0
Marketing and agro-industries	57.2	2.9
Agricultural research and extension	34.4	1.7
Fishing	61.7	3.1
Forestry	31.5	1.6
Others	5.6	0.3
Total	$1,975.9	100.0

Source: IDB report, Participation of the Bank in the Development of Agriculture in Latin America, April 1976.

A number of loans have been concerned with animal health, primarily as part of a determined effort to eradicate foot-and-mouth disease of cattle in South America. Loans to Colombia and Venezuela in 1971 represented a planned program throughout the Southern Hemisphere to control, and eventually eliminate, this economically costly disease. In 1976, a loan to improve dairy production for Mexico City was approved, which included provisions for removing diseased cows from the area and importing higher quality cows to upgrade herds being established in the disease free area.

During recent years, IDB has supported agricultural research activities of three major international centers in Latin America by grants through the Consultative Group for International Agricultural Research (see chapter 7). This money has also gone to strengthen outreach programs of the research centers in Colombia, Mexico, and Peru. In addition, the IDB has recently undertaken preinvestment surveys of agricultural research capabilities in other member countries, with a view toward strengthening national agricultural research institutions.

Progress in production has raised problems of marketing agricultural commodities; consequently, marketing considerations are becoming increasingly important elements of each loan. The IDB is seeking to work with member countries identifying needs and opportunities to make loans dealing with integrated marketing processes.

IDB has been exploring other subsectors of agriculture to determine possibilities for productive investments. Two of these—fisheries and forestry—have been explored in some depth to determine the policy criteria and guidelines for IDB investments in these fields. Loans prepared in accordance with these policies are under active consideration. Several preinvestment studies and project preparation efforts, financed from technical assistance funds, offer possibilities for future funding.

IDB has begun conducting agricultural sector studies in key subsectors, such as marketing and agro-industries, to identify projects consistent with national development priorities which could be considered by financing institutions, including the IDB.

During 1975, the IDB instituted a major review of its agricultural programs in order to determine whether the allocation of resources was consistent with its overall development strategy, and how the flow of resources to the agricultural sector might be improved. Within IDB, lending to agriculture is classified by country and subsector. Countries are classified as A, B, C, or D, according to size and strength of economy, and terms for IDB lending as well as technical assistance are handled accordingly. The group of A countries includes Argentina, Brazil, Mexico, and Venezuela, and the IDB review found that for the 5-year period 1970-74, these had borrowed $557 million, or 65 percent of the $860 million in loans approved for agriculture. Out of the Bank's total lending of $1.672 billion for agriculture during the period 1961-74, Mexico alone had received over $606 million for its agriculture sector. A similar proportion of loans was in prospect for 1975. The B, C, and D countries received little more than 30 percent of overall agricultural lending in 1970-74, but they benefited from 50 percent of the foreign exchange resources lent from FSO on concessional terms.

Partly as a result of its agricultural sector review, the IDB has moved to direct a larger proportion of its resources for agriculture to the B, C, and D countries, particularly those in greatest need. It has also begun to develop more integrated agricultural development projects in order to benefit the conditions of life generally for the poorer rural sectors. Both of these tendencies will mean increased effort by IDB personnel per dollar of funds loaned, since more projects with smaller average size loans will be required to meet the conditions of the smaller countries and those able to absorb only projects of relatively smaller scale. The pipeline of projects for the years 1976-77 now shows that B, C, and D countries would receive about 69 percent of total agricultural sector loans (compared to 44 percent during 1961-74). Integrated agricultural and rural development projects will rise to 27 percent of the total for the years 1976-77, compared to 11 percent during 1961-74. The levels of technical assistance will also increase because the lesser developed countries in the region will require more help in project formulation and implementation.

Technical Cooperation

The Inter-American Development Bank provides resources for technical assistance for the preparation and implementation of financial projects. Most of the technical cooperation is for projects in the lesser developed countries and particularly for agricultural projects. In 1975, IDB provided $25 million for technical assistance; some 33 percent went to the poorer countries in the hemisphere and almost 50 percent was earmarked for agriculture and rural development projects.

The IDB provides technical cooperation in several ways: (1) nonreimbursable, (2) contingent-recovery, and (3) as part of project loans. Technical assistance on a nonreimbursable basis is usually for general or preinvestment studies and support for training or other institutional support. When technical assistance is provided on a contingent-recovery basis, it is usually in connection with preinvestment studies. If, as a result of the study, a project is financed by the IDB, then the cost of the technical help is included in the loan and reimbursement to IDB is made as part of the loan repayment. Technical assistance on a nonreimbursable and contingency basis is handled by a division for technical cooperation within the IDB.

The larger part of technical cooperation is provided, however, as an integral part of loan projects. Many projects which IDB finances require not only "hardware" such as irrigation machinery, but also "software" such as training in land and water management. As IDB seeks to reach the poorer rural sectors in the countries served, it finds increasing need to provide assistance for project implementation. Therefore, projects often include provision for hiring consultants on a short-term or resident basis to provide the implementing institution of recipient countries some technical or managerial support. For example, a loan of $3.7 million to the National Credit Bank of Nicaragua had $400,000 earmarked for hiring experts in agronomy, veterinary medicine, animal feeding, dairy farm operations, and business planning. These consultants helped assure that the credits extended to smaller livestock operators would be useful and the loans would likely be repaid.

Financial assistance through its Preinvestment Fund or Project Preparation Programs or by means of technical assistance is offered by the Bank to help countries identify projects and prepare them for IDB or some other financing institution. IDB is also increasingly active as executing agency of UNDP grants for project identification and preinvestment surveys.

To implement the project after it is approved, the IDB will often assign (using resources of the loan) one or two experts to provide continued surveillance at the country level. Experts may also be sent to the field in the course of a project to study ways of raising working capital or take other steps necessary to permit the project to be executed in accordance with the terms of the loan contract and to meet its objectives.

Another area of technical assistance includes broad sector surveys not related to a specific project. These surveys are done at the request of member countries to provide information for development plans and possible investment by IDB or other lending institutions. The most recently completed studies of this kind involved agricultural surveys conducted by joint FAO/IDB teams in several lesser developed member countries to identify key fields of investment necessary to increase agricultural productivity.[3]

For 1975, technical cooperation on a nonreimbursable and contingent-recovery basis was particularly evident in:

● Greater IDB support for national agencies engaged in project identification, preparation, and evaluation.

● Larger sums for operations in the agricultural sector, including support for international and national agricultural research centers located in Latin America.

● More support for regional operations as compared to strictly national ones.

● A greater number of short-term technical cooperation projects to solve specific problems arising in the Bank's activities with member countries.

Reflecting its increased efforts to strengthen agriculture in developing member countries, IDB held a major seminar on agricultural policy as a limiting factor in the development process. The 5-day seminar in March 1975 in Washington was designed to help institutions in member countries develop suitable policies for agricultural and livestock development and to seek further IDB resources in meeting these objectives. Some 20 experts spoke on diverse aspects of agricultural policy, and proceedings were published by IDB. Similarly, to further encourage member country interest in their agriculture sectors and in IDB assistance, IDB published and distributed in 1976 a brochure discussing its agriculture sector program activities.

International Group for Agricultural Development in Latin America

Background

Leaders in both North and South America who are concerned with the world food situation have often noted the great potential of Latin America to contribute to its own and to world food needs and have considered means to better realize this potential. The Inter-American Development Bank, as a result of its 1974 review of food and agricultural programs in the region, considered ways in which it could do more in agricultural development. Two factors were evident: first, other international organizations were also increasing their activities in this sector and hence coordination was important; second, there were kinds of activities in which several international organizations might usefully work together. Out of these explorations came the idea of a consultative group associated with IDB to further agricultural development in the region.

---

[3]As a means of augmenting its capacity to provide technical assistance, IDB has development agreements with FAO, the Inter-American Institute of Agricultural Sciences (IICA), USDA, and Israel. Also, in 1976, the IDB began a program of supporting technical cooperation between developing country members of the Bank.

During the fall of 1975 and spring of 1976, a series of preparatory
eetings was held in Washington; they were hosted by IDB and chaired by
he provisional Secretariat of the International Group for Agricultural
evelopment in Latin America (IGAD). Attending the meetings were
epresentatives from the principal international organizations, namely the
orld Bank, UNDP, the Economic Commission for Latin America (ECLA)
AO, OAS and its agricultural arm—the Inter-American Institute for
gricultural Sciences—and the CGFPI. The United States was represented,
rimarily by officers from AID, and the Canadian International Development
gency was also represented.

Since the IDB had a principal role in organizing the new institution, it
ought and received support for it from its Board of Governors during their
eeting in 1975.

Organization and Operations

As presently planned, IGAD would have a small secretariat which would
be responsible for calling and servicing meetings of its constituent agencies.
The secretariat would not constitute an operating organization itself, but
would look to its constituent institutional members to carry out, individually
or collectively, specific studies or program activities agreed upon.

Policy guidance for IGAD's program of work would come primarily from
the international organizations that have participated in the preparatory
meetings and which constitute the "International Group" in IGAD's name.
Institutional membership in the group is self-selecting and members are
viewed as potential donor agencies; they provide the budget for the IGAD
secretariat and the financial and other support that may be necessary for
specific projects.

Another source of policy guidance for IGAD is the representatives of the
agricultural ministries and others from the Latin America and Caribbean area.
It is anticipated that member countries will meet as an annual assembly to
review IGAD's work and to offer ideas on the program and on new areas of
activity. The first such assembly was convened in May 1976, at the time of
IDB's Board of Governors' meeting in Cancun, Mexico. At this meeting,
agricultural representatives concurred in IGAD's program activities and some
made additional suggestions. It was agreed that IGAD's principal functions
would be to:

• Study proposed new approaches to technical and financial assistance
for food and agricultural development in the Western Hemisphere,
• Channel a greater flow of external capital and technical cooperation to
the region for food production and rural development, and
• Coordinate food and agricultural development programs of the
international agencies in the region.

It was further agreed that for the immediate future, IGAD's program of work would be:

- Manpower training, particularly for development and implementation of agricultural projects,
- Building linkages between the international research centers, national research institutions, and extension services to the farmer, and
- Reducing postharvest losses (this activity was given priority for the first year's work).

A 3-year budget of $1.15 million was approved to provide for the small secretariat and for necessary consultants. Of this sum, about 65 percent is covered by IDB. Some additional funding and/or borrowing of technical personnel from constituent donor agencies is anticipated to permit IGAD to undertake its coordinating role in each of the areas of work agreed upon, and provide some technical input.

9. ASIAN DEVELOPMENT BANK

Background

Sponsored by the United Nations Economic Commission for Asia and the Far East (ECAFE), the Asian Development Bank (ADB) was established on November 24, 1966, and began operations on December 19, 1966, in Manila, Philippines. The ADB, whose working language is English, is an autonomous organization, not part of the UN system. Its stated purpose is to lend funds, promote the investment of both private and public capital for development purposes, provide technical assistance to its developing member countries, and hasten economic growth and cooperation in the Asian and Pacific region. Bank resources are applied especially to projects which are not adequately financed through other agencies, and which may be a stimulus to regional economic cooperation.

Organization and Operations

While the Bank was established to serve the ECAFE,[1] membership is open to other developed countries that are members of the United Nations or any of its specialized agencies. Current membership (1976) includes 42 countries—28 regional and 14 nonregional. Of these 42 countries, 25 are classified as developing member countries and are eligible to receive assistance from the ADB. Representatives of all members countries make up the organization's governing body, the Board of Governors, which is composed of a Governor and Alternate Governor for each member country. In most cases, the Governor is the Minister of Finance of the member country.

Organizationally, the Bank consists of the Office of the President, the Office of the Secretary, the Office of the General Counsel, the Operations Department, two projects departments, the Economics Office, Administration Department, Controller's and Treasurer's Departments, Information Office, and Office of the Internal Auditor.

Of these, the Operations Department and projects departments are most closely involved in the lending and technical assistance function while the Economic Office is concerned mainly with research relating to the problems and policies of social and economic development, the methodology used for analytical work in the ADB, and the collection of statistics. The Economic Office is also responsible for carrying out independent postevaluation projects financed by ADB.

In May 1974, the Operations and projects departments were reorganized and the existing Projects Department was divided into two, one responsible

---

[1] The name was recently changed to the Economic and Social Commission for Asia and the Pacific (ESCAP) to include island countries of the South Pacific, namely Cook Islands, Fiji, Gilbert Islands, Papua New Guinea, Solomon Islands, Tonga, and Western Samoa.

mainly for agriculture and agriculture-related sectors and the other primarily for infrastructure development (power, transport, communications, etc.).

At the end of June 1976, the ADB staff totaled 736, representing 33 nationalities. Of this number, 273 were professional staff and 463 supporting staff. Currently, U.S. nationals comprise about 11 percent of the professional staff. The supporting staff is drawn almost exclusively from the host country.

In addition to regular staff, ADB employs consultants for its technical assistance programs and for supplementing its own staff on project appraisals or project implementation review. In connection with technical assistance and UNDP-financed projects, consulting firms are recruited to prepare preliminary investigations and reports concerning feasibility, economic and financial justification, and general layout and design, and to estimate cost of projects, time required for construction, etc.

Where projects agreed upon between the ADB and recipient governments require outside consultants, the Bank helps borrowers select and employ consultants for making detailed engineering designs, preparing analyses of bids, and sometimes for supervising projects for an initial period. In these cases, consultants are selected by borrowers and are drawn from among the qualified personnel of member countries. The ADB maintains information on individual consultants and consulting firms and their qualifications to do studies financed by its grants or UNDP.

The main criteria in selecting consultants are technical qualifications and experience for performing the required services. In addition, an effort is made to involve consulting firms from as many member countries as possible and preference is given to qualified local consultants or firms employing consultants from developing member countries.

While Bank operations consist principally of financing specific projects to foster economic growth and cooperation among developing member countries, its limited resources, in comparison with the needs of these countries, require judicious selection of projects. A general review of a country's economic development, with emphasis on aspects of the national and sectoral development programs, is therefore a prerequisite to the selection of projects. After confirming that a project justifies investment, the ADB undertakes technical, economic, and financial evaluations of the project. Only those projects with sufficient economic justification are considered for financing. The Bank is also concerned with overall financial arrangements for a project, including finances contributed to the project by a recipient government. In the case of a revenue-earning project, an appropriate financial return must be evidenced. Since the governments of recipient countries either receive or guarantee the loans, not all types of revenue-earning projects need to show a high rate of financial return. Projects are, however, expected to be technically and organizationally sound. In this connection, the Bank provides technical assistance, either on a reimbursable or grant basis, to help its developing member countries identify and implement projects. The Bank considers all sectors of a country's economy in the process of project selection, but the requirements of a country's development strategy may lead to emphasis at times on some particular sectors or areas.

Postevaluation of Projects

In its evaluation of development projects, the Bank attempts to assess results and the means employed to achieve them. Postevaluation is conducted after disbursement for a project is completed and after it has been in operation for some time. Responsibility for evaluation rests with the Economics Office; reports on its evaluations are made directly to the President and to the Operations Department as well as the country involved in the project.

The purpose of postevaluation is twofold: first, to determine whether a development project has achieved its intended objective, and second, to reexamine the objectives themselves and the means employed to achieve them, in order to improve the quality of the Bank's development projects. The postevaluation program consists of the following efforts:

(1) A project performance audit is performed after completion of Bank-assisted projects to determine whether projects have achieved their stated objectives, and the reasons for deviation, if any.

(2) Intensive studies are carried out on a selected basis; preference is given to difficult and complex projects and to sectors where Bank activities are expected to expand. Such studies serve both the auditing and management function.

(3) Sectoral and country reviews are made based on a large sample of Bank-assisted projects in a country or sector. These are performed to assess the effectiveness and significance of the Bank's operations in a country or sector. Such studies may include some, if not all, of the projects which already have been examined under (1) and (2) above. Moreover, the social and economic impact of the projects as a group can best be assessed over a period of time.

(4) External evaluation is periodically performed by reputable academic or nonprofit organizations engaged to conduct fully independent postevaluation studies. This is not based on any mistrust of the Bank's capacity to evaluate projects, but on the sound principle that any organization will stand to benefit from the application of outside talent to an evaluation of its operations.

Financial Operations

Capitalization and Regular Loans

Ordinary capital resources are made up of capital stock subscribed to by member countries and the funds the ADB raises through the sale of bonds in world money markets. On June 30, 1976, authorized capital stock was $3.676 billion. The subscribed capital was $3.202 billion. Of the amount subscribed, 33 percent was paid-in shares, the latter usually payable in installments and 67 percent of the amount subscribed was in callable shares. The U.S. subscription in June 1976 was $361.9 million. The Board of Directors is currently considering a proposal for the Board of Governors which would increase the Bank's authorized capital by 135 percent, to enable it to meet its lending target in 1977 and beyond.

During 1975, the Bank raised $322.8 million (equivalent) in eight borrowings—more than the total borrowing up to the end of 1974. Borrowings in 1976, up to September 3, totaled a further $507.2 million. The borrowings were accomplished through the sale of bonds and notes in the United States, Japan, Saudi Arabia, Switzerland, Germany, and the Netherlands.

Concessional Lending

Since 1968, when the Multi-Purpose Special Fund was established, the Bank has endeavored to meet the needs of its poorer and less developed countries for loan financing on concessional terms. The special fund consisted of resources contributed on a voluntary basis, in addition to some funds set aside from the Bank's paid-in capital. In 1974, the Asian Development Fund was created to consolidate all the concessional funds, with the exception of the Technical Assistance Special Fund. Contributions to the new Asian Development Fund totaled $590 million from 13 developed member countries, including $100 million from the United States. Loans from the fund have been standardized on terms of 40 years maturity and a service charge of 1 percent per annum. Eligibility of member countries for such loans is determined by the Board of Directors, based mainly on the country's economic situation.

At the end of 1975, total loan commitments from concessional funds amounted to $651 million, leaving a balance of only $40 million, so an early replenishment of the Asian Development Fund became imperative if the objective of increasing concessional lending was to be achieved. Following several meetings of potential donors, a target of $830 million was set to cover the 3-year period 1976-78 and approved by the Board of Governors in December 1975. This amount was subject to adjustment of certain countries' contributions, and it was later reduced to $809 million. The projected U.S. contribution over the 3-year period, subject to Congressional appropriation, is $180 million. By June 30, 1976, commitments totaling $477 million to the fund's replenishment had been received and the replenishment went into effect.

Similar criteria are used in selecting projects financed from ordinary capital resources and from the concessional funds. Generally, projects are selected which have a distinct and justifiable priority in the development plans of the countries concerned and which may generate substantial economic and/or social benefits, though not always direct financial or foreign exchange returns. Because of the state of development and needs of the developing countries in Asia, concessional fund loans have been made predominantly (46 percent) in agriculture and agriculture-related sectors. In 1975, a total of $166 million was given in 14 concessional loans to six

100

countries. In 1976, the lending target for agricultural projects was $250 million.

Development Assistance in Agriculture

Loan Operations

Bank participation in loans for agricultural development has grown sharply over the past few years. Because of the importance of agriculture in most Asian economies, the ADB undertook a regional agricultural survey in 1967. Since the survey's completion in 1968, the ADB has progressively expanded its activities in the agriculture and agro-industry sector. The share of agriculture and agro-industry in Bank lending jumped from 24.5 percent in 1974 to 37.2 percent in 1975. That year, 14 loans totaling $245.9 million were approved in the agro-industry and agriculture sector. Of these, four totaling $56.1 million were for irrigation and area development, two totaling $33.2 million were for fisheries, four totaling $110 million were for fertilizer projects, and three totaling $37.1 million were for jute and palm oil processing. Through 1975, ADB had approved nearly $590 million in loans for 64 agriculture-related projects. Over half the total amount lent for agriculture and agro-industry has been financed on concessional terms.

Following a decision of the Board of Directors in February 1975, a task force is currently undertaking the second Asian Agricultural Survey, to help ADB formulate its future role in contributing to the development of the regional rural economy. A report on this second agricultural survey is expected to be made by the end of 1976.

Agriculture also dominates the Bank's technical assistance activities; over 40 percent of the Bank's technical assistance projects at regional and national levels have gone to agriculture and agro-industry.

Assistance has also been given to support agricultural research in the region. ADB has made direct grants to research institutions (notably the Asian Vegetable Research and Development Center, the International Rice Research Institute, and the International Crops Research Institute for the Semi-Arid Tropics) and has incorporated research facilities and programs as integral parts of agricultural investment projects. Funds granted to international research institutions through June 1976 total $1.3 million.

Agricultural education and training components have been built into many projects in the agricultural sector. In addition, a regional seminar on agriculture and a regional workshop on irrigation and water management have been conducted and a seminar on agricultural credit was held late in 1976.

Technical Assistance

During the first 2 years of the Bank's operations, technical assistance was limited to assistance of an advisory nature. Technical assistance for project preparation and implementation began in 1968, and by the end of June 1976, 103 such projects had been approved. Technical assistance activities approved in 1975 totaled $7.0 million as compared to $5.6 million in 1974. Through

1975, $30.86 million had been approved for technical assistance on a grant basis, since the Bank began operations (this sum includes funds extended to the Bank as executing agent for UNDP). Total technical assistance of over $12.0 million was allocated for 83 agricultural projects, both national and regional. Technical assistance projects completed through 1975 total 102, of which 22 were completed in 1975. Countries that received technical assistance in 1975 included Afghanistan, Bangladesh, Burma, Indonesia, Republic of Korea, Laos, Nepal, Pakistan, Papua New Guinea, Philippines, and Western Samoa. Technical assistance by the Bank is particularly important in helping the lesser developed countries in the region it serves.

10. THE AFRICAN DEVELOPMENT BANK

Background

The African Development Bank (AfDB) is a regional effort to improve economic cooperation and foster economic growth among member nations. It was established in September 1964, under auspices of the United Nations Economic Commission for Africa (ECA). A committee of nine states, established by an ECA resolution of 1962, prepared a draft charter for the financial institution. At a meeting of finance ministers at the Khartoum Conference of August 1963, 22 African states signed the protocols establishing the AfDB. The Committee of Nine was then recommissioned to encourage ratification of the agreement by other African states and to draft arrangements and procedures for the Bank's operation. Operations began at headquarters in Abidjan, Ivory Coast, in July 1966. As of January 1976, 41 African nations had been affirmed members. Membership in the Bank is not open to nations outside the region, but outside capital contributions are welcomed through its concessionary lending affiliate, the African Development Fund (AfDF).

The organization's objectives, as stated in the preamable to its articles of incorporation, are "to contribute to the economic development and social progress of its members—individually and jointly." It seeks to provide financing for investment projects and programs, giving priority to those that will benefit more than one African state and further inter-African trade and economic integration of the region. To accomplish these ends, the AfDB works to mobilize and coordinate both African and non-African financial resources, and to provide technical assistance to member countries for study, preparation, and execution of projects and programs.

Organization, Operations, and Finances

There are five operating divisions: Preinvestment Division, Operations epartment, Finance Department, Legal Office, and Office of the Secretary eneral. The Operations Department is divided into three divisions: Loans, rojects, and Economics. The Preinvestment Division is operated jointly with he UNDP. Although the AfDB is not a part of the specialized agencies, it has special agreement with FAO and UNESCO for project identification and reparation in agriculture and education.

Bank staff is drawn primarily from member countries in Africa. It often dds expertise to its operations through the use of consultants; the Bank ncourages·the creation of African consulting firms and turns to them as well s others for needed external assistance.

Through the reporting period ending December 31, 1975, the authorized apital of the Bank was equal to $480 million, of which half was in the form f paid-in capital and half was in the form of callable capital shares.

Like the other international development banks, voting power is linked to country's capital subscription. In the AfDB, no nation has as much as 10 ercent of the voting strength. Nigeria, Libya, Algeria, and Egypt are the four argest capital subscribers. Subscriptions are allocated among the members using a formula that takes into account population, gross national product (GNP), foreign trade, and balance of payments. In each case, half the amount of capital subscribed to is paid in (in either gold or convertible currencies) and the remainder is callable, should it be necessary.

The AfDB does not seek to compete with private banks in financing projects. It gives priority to projects which may be integral parts of national or regional development plans. In placing loans, it usually charges interest at about 7 to 8 percent with maturities of 5 to 20 years. These terms are usually better than the borrowing entities may obtain from commercial financial institutions.

To conserve its capital and ensure adequate local involvement in the proposed project, the AfDB requires that 40 percent of the project funds be provided from sources in the borrowing country. It has also set an upper limit on the size of any one project loan, in order to broaden its base of operations while staying within its limited resources. In 1975, no loan was made for more than $6 million.

The Bank has rapidly increased the tempo of its commitments. In 1975, it approved 28 loans totaling $103.6 million. This compares with the 1974 commitments of $88.6 million and the 1973 commitments of $42.7 million. Actual disbursements in 1975 were a record $48 million, twice the 1974 amount of $22.9 million.

African Development Fund

The African Development Fund (AfDF) is the concessional lending affiliate of the African Development Bank. The fund is designed to channel non-African resources into the African development process and to help meet the need for softer terms for projects in African nations that could not borrow at the regular terms offered by the AfDB.

The fund membership includes 12 European countries, Canada, Brazil Japan, Saudi Arabia, and the AfDB itself, representing all of its membe states. In 1976, the U.S. Congress appropriated $15 million for a U.S contribution to the fund and the United States expected to become member before the end of CY 1976.

With the U.S. contribution, total resources pledged to the fund ar expected to amount to about $410 million. A number of member states hav yet to formally ratify replenishment pledges which are included in this figure When all pledges are ratified, however, fund resources will have increased b 310 percent since 1973.

The growth in the fund's lending activities has been consistent with th growth in its resources. In CY 1974, the first full year of operation, AfD lending totaled $46.2 million. In 1975, the rate of lending almost double reaching $92 million. The fund expects to lend $100 million in CY 197 and plans to increase the figure again in 1977. All loans carry a service charg of .75 percent per annum on the disbursed amount with a repayment perio of 50 years, including a 10-year grace period. The fund has concentrate primarily on the development of agriculture and transportation, but has als been active in lending to the public utility, health, and education sectors.

Development Assistance in Agriculture

The performance of the agricultural sector varies among African countries but most suffer from low productivity. At the same time, the vast majority of people in Africa are engaged in agricultural pursuits and their earnings remain low. Hence the Bank has given high priority to assisting the agricultural sector of its member countries. The African countries themselves have become increasingly aware of the importance of agriculture in overall development and of the need to invest in agricultural modernization.

In recent years, a large portion of the Bank's assistance in the agricultural sector has been provided through the African Development Fund on concessional terms. In 1975, the fund gave $32.2 million, or 35 percent of its commitments, to agriculture. The cumulative commitments of the fund to agriculture are $58.9 million, or 42 percent of its commitments. The Bank itself has a cumulative allocation of $36 million to agriculture or 11.4 percent of its investments on regular terms. An apparent decrease in 1975 of the Bank's support of agricultural projects through regular loans, compared to the historic proportion of AfDB loans to agriculture, represents a shift to more concessional lending through the fund. The Bank made only two loans out of regular funds to the agricultural sector in 1975. One was to Gabon for $4.8 million to rehabilitate and develop cocoa plantations. The other, to Ghana for $3.8 million, was for mechanized cotton production.

Loans granted through the fund were varied. It gave $5.5 million to a palm oil development project in the Central African Republic, which included a plantation development phase and later a crushing plant to process oil. In Chad, $5.1 million was committed to a project that would bring 5,000 hectares under irrigation and also provide rice storage facilities. Ethiopia was granted a loan for $5.3 million for livestock development; this project also included World Bank concessional financing by IDA. The project includes range management, extension services, and road development. Other projects financed by the African Development Fund include development of 6,700 hectares of rice land in Mali and an irrigation scheme in Somalia.

At the end of 1975, the Bank had identified 95 agricultural projects with a potential financing value of about $337.7 million. It increased the number of its identification missions over previous years and has held meetings with other financial and development institutions in order to build up a pipeline of appropriate projects. Hence the Bank expects to increase its assistance in agriculture.

Private Financing Through the AfDB

In 1970, the Bank established a private development finance company, the Societé International pour les Investissements et le Development en Afrique (SIFIDA) to attract development financing from non-African financial institutions for private enterprises in Africa. SIFIDA shareholders are commercial banks and private corporations in Western Europe, Japan, and the United States. There are eight U.S. shareholders who have about 12.5 percent of the equity in SIFIDA.

In March 1975, the Association of African Development Finance

Institutions was established at a meeting attended by most African national development banks. This marked the fruition of initiatives taken by the AfDB in 1970 to coordinate efforts of the national development banks in Africa. Provisionally, the AfDB serves as the association's secretariat. Its membership includes 50 institutions, of which 44 are from 30 African states. Its activities provide for staff training for member countries and information exchange on technical and financial matters.

11. ORGANIZATION OF AMERICAN STATES

Background

The charter of the Organization of American States (OAS) was signed at Bogota, Colombia, in 1948 and modified by a Protocol approved in a special conference in Buenos Aires in 1967. The longstanding concern of the OAS and its predecessor organizations with the problems of agricultural development is evidenced by the creation of the Inter-American Institute of Agricultural Sciences (IICA) in 1942, and the convening of the First Inter-American Conference on Agriculture as far back as 1930. The principal work of agricultural development within the OAS system has been carried out by the General Secretariat and the Inter-American Institute for Agricultural Sciences. IICA is one of the specialized organizations within the purview of the OAS General Assembly.

Within the General Secretariat, agricultural development of member countries is aided by activities of the Inter-American Economic and Social Council and the Inter-American Council for Education, Science, and Culture. Both councils carry on their operations through secretariats that include technical staff for conducting studies and providing technical assistance for agricultural development.

In addition to agencies associated with the OAS, the Western Hemisphere countries receive assistance for agricultural development from subregional banks, as well as from the Inter-American Development Bank. Also, the regional bodies of the UN system operate programs in the Hemisphere countries. Figure 7 indicates the relationship of these several other international agencies as well as the principal units of the OAS system.

Inter-American Institute of Agricultural Sciences

In its early years, IICA was concerned primarily with agricultural research and training, and was headquartered at Turrialba in Costa Rica. For almost two decades after its founding, it carried on a wide range of agronomic experiments and trials and also was involved in research on livestock improvement. During these years, it offered training leading to graduate degrees as well as specialized courses without degree orientation. In 1951 IICA conducted a broad, external review of its program in the light of the new concepts of development and the advances in agricultural research that had occurred in Latin American countries since its founding. As a result of this review, the member governments decided that the organization should concentrate efforts in several principal lines of action, providing development assistance to all member states in the Hemisphere, and that it should put emphasis on strengthening national institutions. IICA remained head-quartered in Costa Rica, but in 1960 moved its offices from Turrialba to San Jose, and in 1976 constructed its new headquarters on the edge of that city.[1] Also, in 1973, a new convention recognizing the changes in the Institute's

---

[1]The research center continued at Turrialba as a separate institution.

(Partial Listing)

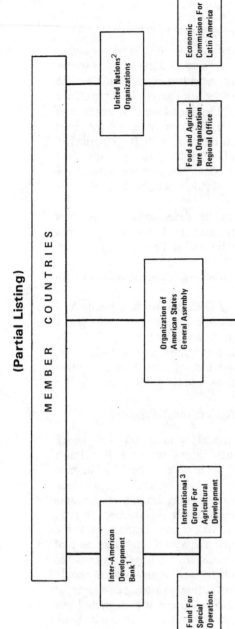

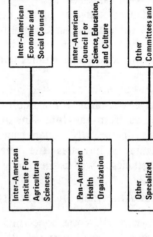

MEMBER COUNTRIES

United Nations[2] Organizations

Food and Agriculture Organization Regional Office

Economic Commission For Latin America

Organization of American States General Assembly

Inter-American Economic and Social Council

Inter-American Institute For Agricultural Sciences

Inter-American Council For Science, Education, and Culture

Pan-American Health Organization

Other Committees and Councils

Other Specialized Organizations

Inter-American Development Bank[1]

International[3] Group For Agricultural Development

Fund For Special Operations

[1]In addition to IDB, there are other regional development banks serving countries in a limited area e.g., Carribbean Development Bank, Central American Development Bank.
[2]World wide organizations of the United Nations System operate regional offices to serve the Western Hemisphere countries.
[3]This is a new organization sponsored by IDB with support from IBRD, UNDP and USAID.

programs and activities was written and submitted to IICA member governments. This convention has not yet been ratified.

Organization and Operations

IICA is governed by a Board of Directors made up of representatives of 25 countries in the Western Hemisphere. Canada became a member in 1973 and several Caribbean countries have also gained membership in recent years. The Board of Directors is nominally made up of country representatives or Ambassadors to the OAS, which meets in Washington. However, since that body deals with a wide range of political as well as economic and social matters, it has delegated authority to a Board of Directors that meets annually in different member countries. It is this annual Board of Directors that sets operating policies for IICA. A Special Executive Committee composed of 10 country representatives (including the United States) meets twice a year to provide closer attention to programs, budgets, and other aspects of IICA's operation.

Funds for IICA are provided primarily by quota assessments among member countries. These quotas follow the pattern set by OAS; the U.S. share was approximately 66 percent, but with the accession of Canada and the Caribbean countries, it is now some 61 percent. Quota funds amounted to $6.3 million for FY 1975, $7.0 million for FY 1976, and $8.2 million for FY 1977.

In addition to its program that is funded by country quotas, IICA carries on a program of projects under *ad hoc* contracts with specific agencies of member countries and with international development institutions such as the Inter-American Development Bank and the Kellogg Foundation. The level of funding for these projects varies from year to year; it was $4.4 million for FY 1975, $2.5 million for FY 1976, and $2.2 million for FY 1977. From time to time, USAID has asked IICA to undertake *ad hoc* projects under special contracts separate from assessed quotas contributed by the United States.

The allocation of regular (quota) funds by major lines of action during the past 3 years is indicated in table 11.

Program Activities

During the past 5 years, IICA has provided technical cooperation and training in six major lines of action: (1) Operating an information and documentation center, which is also the Latin American arm of FAO's information collection and distribution system in all aspects of food and agricultural development. (2) Strengthening agricultural education; the emphasis on this activity is to help educational institutions improve their teaching practices and the content of their agricultural courses, particularly at the postgraduate level. (3) Increasing the effectiveness of agricultural research programs, by improving the management and technical aspects of agricultural research institutions. (4) Encouraging structural change in agricultural sectors by studying various aspects of rural development, agrarian reform, and peasant organizations. (5) Promoting increased productivity by better farm management practices and the utilization of more advanced technologies. This line of action also includes aid to improve marketing

Table 11—Allocation of IICA resources by program activity, 1975-77

Program activity	FY 1975	FY 1976	FY 1977
	$1,000		
Information on agriculture and rural development	480	664	922
Agricultural education	959	975	722
Agricultural research	659	775	884
Promotion of agricultural production	1,203	1,192	1,488
Promotion of structural change in agriculture	568	621	601
Administration of agricultural policy	685	1,136	1,396
Other program activities	515	297	425
Total program funded (administrative costs not included)	5,069	5,660	6,438

practices for food crops and to reduce postharvest losses. (6) Strengthening the administration of agricultural policy and agricultural institutions.

Most of IICA's work is accomplished by helping focus attention on specific problems or constraints to agricultural development in member countries, by providing technical personnel to work in the agricultural institutions of these countries on short-term or resident basis, by conducting various courses and seminars, and by publishing and disseminating a wide range of agricultural reports.

Examples of work performed during FY 1975 in IICA's major lines of action include the following:

(1) Information on agriculture and rural development: Aid on Argentina's project for the National Agricultural Information and Documentation Service; courses and in-service training in library sciences in Brazil.

(2) Agricultural education: Advisory services to the Faculty of Agronomy of the Bolivian University at Ururo; course on methodology for professors of the Inter-American rural photography center, Colombia.

(3) Agricultural research: Updating the Directory of Agricultural Research Institutions in the Southern Zone; advisory services to the Forest Research Institution in Bolivia; lectures in plant physiology at the Federal University of Rio Grande de Sul, Brazil; national meeting on forest plantation projects, Bogota, Colombia.

(4) Promotion of agricultural production: International seminar on drip irrigation; seminar on production systems; first national meeting on marketing systems, storage centers, and wholesale markets, Bolivia; courses on the management of small irrigated properties, Petrolina, Brazil.

(5) Promotion of structural change in agriculture: Training in campesino community enterprises for Paraguay; in-service training fellowships on rural development, Teresina, Brazil.

(6) Administration of agricultural policy: Advisory service for the National Economic and Planning Council, Bolivia; counsel on preparation, analysis, and selection of development alternatives for the agricultural sector of Rio Grande de Sul, Brazil.

In addition to its principal program actions, IICA engages in a number of closely related activities designed to increase the importance that member states attach to agriculture and rural development in their countries. An important vehicle for this is the annual medals awarded by IICA for outstanding service and achievement in agriculture within the hemisphere. One medal is awarded for outstanding scientific accomplishment; one for outstanding contributions in rural development; and a third for professionals under 35 who have made outstanding contributions to agriculture.

Simon Bolivar Fund

A new element in IICA funding was introduced in 1975 when Venezuela pledged to contribute $10 million over a period of 5 years to establish the Simon Bolivar Fund in support of the Institute's program. This grant prompted some additional, though small, contributions from other Latin American countries so that a program budget of almost $2.8 million was available for the first year's operation. Although the Venezuelan grant and some of the other early contributions were in convertible currencies, provisions of the Fund permit payments in local currencies as well. All contributions to the the Fund are voluntary.

The work program of the Fund is formulated and administered in the same way as the general program of the Institute. For the first operating year, 1976, the program gives priority to three existing lines of action carried out by IICA: helping to increase agricultural production and productivity, promoting structural change in rural areas, and improving the administration of agricultural policies and institutions.

Agricultural Programs in the OAS Secretariat

At present, OAS has a wide range of activities related to agriculture, including programs in research, technical assistance, and training, which are the responsibility of either the Economic and Social Council or the Scientific,

Educational, and Cultural Council. Their programs are described briefly below.

Agricultural Programs in the Secretariat for Economic and Social Affairs

The agricultural programs in the Office of Economic and Social Affairs are carried on through its Rural and Urban Development Program and the Regional Development Program. The Rural and Urban Development Program covers research on specific problems as well as on the agricultural sector as a whole; projects in technical assistance are provided directly by the staff or external experts, and training is offered in specialized OAS centers or by *ad hoc* courses in institutions of member countries.

The programs include two types of research, one related to activities of the Permanent Executive Committee of the Inter-American Social and Economic Council (CEPCIES), previously called the Inter-American Committee of the Alliance for Progress (CIAP), and the other oriented toward analyses of particular aspects of agricultural development.

CEPCIES makes periodic reviews at the request of governments in which an overall evaluation of the agricultural sector, recent developments, and short-run and medium-term projections are made. These in-depth reviews deal with the main aspects of the agricultural sector. Followup reviews, usually made after several years, serve to update previous studies. Usually six in-depth country studies are undertaken each year along with two or three followup and intermediate studies. As a result, each country should receive an in-depth study every 3 years. Sometimes these analyses are made on a regional basis: groups of countries with common characteristics or problems requiring coordination in their solution are studied together.

Research projects not directly related to CEPCIES reviews are conducted on special aspects of agricultural development representing serious problems at the regional level, or those which, although referring to a particular country, can shed light on similar problems in other countries. Studies of this kind are often presented as background material or proposed position papers before appropriate organs of the OAS system, and lead to general recommendations to the member countries or joint declarations of policy. Recent examples of this type of research are the studies on the state of Latin American agriculture, strategies for rural development for the 1970's, use of fertilizers in several countries, effect of currency overvaluation of agricultural trade and production, the agricultural economy of Colombia, and agrarian reform as related to resource distribution and agricultural productivity.

Technical assistance is provided to member countries at their request, and the assistance in agriculture often has high priority in national programs. These country programs are evaluated through a formal procedure, using as a main criterion the conclusions reached in the CEPCIES country reviews. Assistance is granted according to the availability of resources. The Secretariat for Economic and Social Affairs conducts an average of six technical missions in agriculture a year, which represent some 50 man-months. About 10 percent of this work is done by staff members.

Recent examples include a mission on hydrology and another on sugarcane crop mechanization, both pertinent to an ongoing project in horticulture; a mission on agricultural extension; one on regional agricultural planning; and another on agricultural marketing.

Training opportunities in agriculture are provided in various countries, particularly in Europe, the United States, and Israel, where knowledge in some specific agricultural matters of importance for Latin American countries has advanced to a high level. The role of the OAS Secretariat for Development Cooperation is to pinpoint specific needs for training, and to identify the training facilities in more advanced countries.

The OAS is currently involved in 11 agricultural courses, including agricultural planning, artificial insemination, and fruit crop technology. These courses are offered with varying frequency in line with requests received.

The Rural and Urban Development Program includes rural development activities particularly oriented toward specific problems. A relatively new program, its main instrument has been the joint OAS/Israel/IDB Project which is providing interested countries interdisciplinary teams of experts to guide and train national technicians in the formulation and execution of rural development plans and investment projects for integrated rural development.

Another objective of the Rural and Urban Development Program is to strengthen cooperatives, as well as the government agencies responsible for promoting them as a means of improving rural life. During 1975, technical assistance missions in several countries conducted nine courses and five seminars, and provided training to over 100 Latin American technicians.

The Regional Development Program, also within the Secretariat for Economic and Social Affairs, approaches agricultural development from the viewpoint of identifying potential resources, designing techniques and methodologies for resource evaluation, formulating projects for use at the regional rather than the national level, and establishing provisions for their sound administration. The agricultural program constitutes almost 40 percent of this unit's resources. Programs are carried on in two ways: (1) strengthening institutional capacity in the member countries through technical assistance to national organizations involved in resource development and training of local technicians, and (2) providing technical assistance in surveys to determine development possibilities in selected regions such as river basins.

The Regional Development Program also provides some training through an inter-American program for project evaluation and formulation, offering courses on subjects such as soils, geology, hydrology, survey of underground waters, utilization of forest resources, and administration of integrated natural resource surveys. About 100 Latin American technicians benefit from these courses annually. A project in formal adademic training in economics and natural resource management is being carried on by the regional development unit in cooperation with U.S. universities.

An increase in agricultural development work, particularly in water resource projects and in the conservation, development, and administration of forest resources, is contemplated. The unit's work in agriculture will emphasize help to national planning organizations in determining data needs and survey design, interpreting survey results, gathering data on natural resources, and preparing long-term plans on the research required to implement established policies on regional development. The establishment of a regional facility for natural resource development training will help accomplish these objectives. Work in agro-industries is carried on in another unit of the Secretariat for Economic and Social Affairs.

Agricultural Programs in the Secretariat for Education, Science and Cultural Affairs

The principal activity of this secretariat in the field of agriculture is the Multinational Project on Agricultural Sciences. Started in 1968, this project seeks to provide the Latin American countries with training, research capability, and technical assistance to overcome technical and scientific barriers confronting the agricultural sector. The agricultural sciences project is carried on through several national institutions in countries with high levels of experience in certain fields. Project supported courses in nutrition, animal genetics, soil, grazing, breeding, statistics, and microbiology have provided over 300 man-months of training, plus equipment, during the years since 1968.

12. EMERGING ISSUES AND INSTITUTIONAL ARRANGEMENTS

Recent years have brought a heightened awareness of the economic interdependence of nations and the need to make that interdependence a basis of mutually advantageous adjustment rather than a source of confrontation and conflict. International organizations described in this report have had an important role in the process of political and economic adjustment. Sometimes, the secretariats and bureaucracies of the international organizations have advanced the process of accomodation, while national representatives have confronted each other with nonnegotiable position papers. Often, however, the international forums have appeared to be scenes of confrontation rather than accommodation.

Although the UN General Assembly seems to have lost some of its usefulness as an instrument for reconciling international political differences, the UN specialized agencies have grown more important as a forum and focal point for discussing economic development issues. Developing countries have recognized the value of their preponderant voting power within the UN system to orient its policies and programs toward their economic development. Industrialized countries, including the United States, have recognized the value of international forums as means of moderating differences on economic issues among member countries. And there is recognition that the international organizations can channel development assistance that is more consistent with the evolving political independence of developing countries.

Goals and Targets—Development Assistance or a New International Economic Order

The most broadly based international development goals are those enunciated by the United Nations for the Second Development Decade—the 1970's. While stated in general social and economic terms, the development goals set by the UN do carry implications for the agriculture sectors of industrialized as well as developing countries. The targets include growth rates for the economies and agricultural sectors of developing countries, improvements in the pattern of trade to benefit developing countries, and levels of assistance from donor countries to facilitate the attainment of these targets. The language of the Second Development Decade statements follows concepts and measures that had been used for more than a decade by donor and recipient countries alike. However, while adhering to the strategies and targets of the Second Development Decade, the Sixth Special Session of the UN General Assembly on May 1, 1974, adopted, without vote, the idea of a new international economic order which calls for significantly different relationships in the international economic system.

There were many factors which led to the enunciation of a new international economic order, such as increasing nationalism among some developing countries, frustration among many at the slow pace of their development, new hardships precipitated by higher priced oil and food imports, declining export earnings associated with the recession in most industrialized countries, and a decline in the real value of the assistance offered by major donor countries. However, a decisive factor in the tone of the new démarche was the example set by the OPEC countries and the significant increase in their economic and political power resulting from cartel policies on oil.

A UN-appointed Committee for Development Planning[1] was convened in April 1975 to examine critical development issues in connection with a review of progress in the Second Development Decade. Significantly, the committee considered the objectives of the new international economic order, as well as the targets of the Second Development Decade, as a basis for evaluating economic development progress during the 1970's.

Targets of Developing Country Growth
and Donor Country Assistance

The UN committee noted that several of the targets set for the Second Development Decade were being met during 1971-73; however, it found that in the aftermath of the sharp increase in oil prices, the shortfall in food production and subsequent increase in grain prices, and the severe recession and prolonged inflation in the industrialized countries, progress in the developing countries was eroded. Thus, except for the OPEC countries, the situation for most of the developing countries by the end of 1975 was little better than at the beginning of the decade. Indeed, in food and agriculture, the situation had become worse. Although levels of production in 1975-76 in most parts of the developing world were substantially better than in the two earlier years, it was not significantly above long-term trend lines and hence just barely kept abreast of burgeoning populations. Morever, for most developing country exporters of agriculture commodities, the boom enjoyed during 1973-74 was gone in 1975, while the prices of imports, particularly oil and manufactured goods, continued upward so that the terms of trade worsened for them.

Analysis of economic development during the first half of the second decade makes clear that among developing countries, differences in per capita income and economic outlook have grown greater. A new "fourth world" has been identified—some 40 countries that have been most seriously affected by the recent turbulent economic period, and whose resources in relation to population are poor. These countries are preponderantly rural; for the billion or more people who live there, the prospects for better nutrition, and better economic conditions generally, remain dim—particularly in the rural areas.

On targets for donor assistance the situation is also mixed. An aid target of 1 percent of donor country GNP, with 0.7 percent representing official development assistance, was passed by the General Assembly (but not agreed

---

[1]This committee, appointed by the UN Economic and Social Council, is comprised of 23 members from different countries, but appointed in their personal capacity. One U.S. national served on the committee and was reporteur. A report on the committee's work was published in June 1975.

116

to by all donor countries). The target has been referred to in subsequent statements and resolutions of UN agencies. Similarily, the World Food Conference target of $5 billion a year in external development assistance for the food and agriculture sector has been cited on several occasions in other UN forums. Linking development assistance levels to GNP takes into account not only rising wealth but inflation as well. Several smaller donor countries in Europe have accepted and achieved the target on official development assistance.

At the time the target was enunicated, the very substantial transfer of resources to one group of developing countries, namely the OPEC group, could not be taken into account. These transfers represent a resource that can be readily used for development purposes not only in the OPEC countries but others as well. This process is getting underway, particularly among Arab countries, but it is not clear whether these resource transfers will have a significant impact on the economic development of recipient countries.

The several new facilities initiated by the World Bank Group suggest a continued rapid growth in resources from traditional contributors and lenders, for example increased regular and concessional lending levels through the IBRD Third Window, and the IBRD-IMF arrangement on the sale of gold holdings with the proceeds going to the poorest countries. Altogether, the diversity of development assistance flows makes it difficult to determine how close to the target the resource transfers are.

The trade goals set by the UN for the Second Development Decade are for developing countries to increase imports somewhat less than 7 percent and to increase exports by more than 7 percent during the 1970's. Since many of the exports would be agricultural commodities, and since LDC growth in agricultural output is targeted at 4 percent, the increase would affect current trade patterns of developed as well as less developed countries. Hence, some developed countries have questioned the views contained in FAO's study of the international agricultural adjustments necessary to facilitate export growth for less developed countries.[2] In trade targets expressed in the UN's new international economic order, and in recent UNCTAD meetings, the language has become more explicit on means to achieve growth in export earnings for developing countries. The means advocated by many developing countries is for a more managed international trade to accomplish their objectives and less emphasis on market forces. With the example of OPEC in mind, there is increased solidarity among developing countries and a greater willingness to adopt supply and price stabilizing mechanisms for commodities that are of key importance to their foreign exchange earnings.

A New International Economic Order

For some developing countries the issues of external aid and increased trade are surrogates for the real issue of redistributing the world's wealth and creating a new international economic order. While developing countries

---

[2]FAO papers suggest that the international adjustment needed for the less developed countries to attain their export targets might best be accomplished by adjustments in production and marketing by the developed countries, and that tariff and other barriers should be reduced to facilitate this.

differ widely on tactics, they have been impressively united in seeking fundamental changes in economic relationships and in the process by which decisions are made on international economic matters.

The developing country manifesto took the form of two resolutions adopted by the Sixth Special Session of the UN General Assembly in May 1974. One resolution outlines the proposed new relationship between industrialized and developing countries and the second set forth a "Program of Action on the Establishment of a New International Economic Order." The resolutions were adopted with some 200 reservations by 20 Western countries (including Japan, Australia, and the United States). Then in December 1974, in the regular session of the UN General Assembly, a "Charter of Economic Rights and Duties of States" was adopted by a vote of 120 for, 6 against (including the United States), and 10 abstentions. In international forums since then, the United States and other Western governments have continued to express general support for the aspirations of developing countries embodied in these resolutions, but have steadfastly opposed a number of specific provisions.

In the resolutions and subsequent debates on establishing a new economic order, developing countries have endeavored to establish wide-ranging obligations on the part of industrialized countries (and corresponding rights for developing countries) with respect to levels of assistance, for example in fertilizers, food aid, and development assistance; trade, including price and access to markets; investment; transfer of resources and technology; and monetary reform. Among the differences that have been particularly contentious are those dealing with sovereignty over natural resources as this affects the treatment of foreign investment, and transnational corporations. Another has been on the formation of producer organizations (cartels) and the indexation of prices for primary products exported by developing countries with prices of processed goods they import. Other areas of difference arise out of questionable references to colonialism, restitution for alleged wrongdoings, linking of defense expenditures to development financing, etc.

The significance of these UN resolutions for agricultural development lies in the acceptance by international organizations within the UN system that they need to relate their policies and programs to the accomplishment of the goals espoused. The problems and issues raised in pursuance of these goals are different from those associated with improving technology and increasing food production. The UN goals and strategies for the Second Development Decade raise the issue of a UN role in bringing about income transfers from the more developed countries to the less developed and within the latter, from their affluent to their poor. The formulation of socioeconomic goals, and the means to achieve them, are usually handled through each country's own political process, and sovereign nations are reluctant to open up this process to international agencies. Hence, debate is spirited in forums such as the FAO on the subject of agrarian reform, with its implications for structural changes in agricultural economies and equity considerations in agricultural policies. Debates in international forums on changes in the terms of trade are no less spirited, since they too raise issues of equity and of political processes.

118

Trade and Development—UNCTAD

For a number of years those concerned with economic growth of low-income countries have pointed out the interconnection between trade and development (see, for example, *22, 29, 39*). In 1964, a meeting was held in Geneva under UN auspices which addressed itself to these problems. This meeting created permanent machinery within the United Nations to deal with the problems of trade and development—a conference to meet every four years, a Trade and Development Board (TDB) to meet annually, and standing committees of the TDB concerned with commodities, manufacturers, financial issues, and shipping. The TDB, composed of 55 member countries, acts as a continuing governing body and holds several policy meetings each year.

An important outcome of the first UNCTAD meeting (referred to as UNCTAD I) was a new unity among developing countries permitting them to win passage of a set of principles on trade relations, which the United States and most other developed countries have not fully accepted. UNCTAD II was held in New Delhi in 1968 and was preceded by a meeting in Algiers of representatives from 77 less developed countries to plan a common strategy for the conference.[3] While UNCTAD II fell short of their aspirations, it achieved some progress on the major issues before the delegates. A system of generalized preferences for developing countries was formulated. The conference also adopted the UN goal of 1 percent of developed countries' GNP as a reasonable target for net financial transfers to the less developed countries.

UNCTAD III was convened in Santiago in the spring of 1972. It was preceded by a meeting of developing countries in Lima which issued a paper on principles of international economic behavior among developed and developing nations. The work of UNCTAD III was divided among a number of committees and special work groups. In addition to committees on (1) commodities, (2) manufactures, (3) finances, and (4) invisibles (including shipping, tourism, and insurance), two new committees were established—one on trade relations among countries with different economic systems and the second on providing additional assistance for the least developed among the developing countries. Three working groups were also established on (1) institutional arrangements for increasing the effectiveness of UNCTAD, (2) trade among developing countries, and (3) technology transfers.

The trade issue given most attention was LDC participation in negotiations under the General Agreement on Trade and Tariffs (GATT), so they could have a voice in the 1973 sessions and their interests could be taken into account. The developing countries also sought wider agreement on a system of generalized preferences to favor their exports. The questions of LDC diversification, market access, and nontariff barriers affecting the export of commodities from less developed countries to the more affluent countries

---

[3]Thereafter, the developing countries, collectively, were often referred to as the "Group of 77."

were also debated. In addition to reasserting a level of finanical transfers of 1 percent of GNP by the developed countries (and 0.7 percent by official transfers), an issue was made of the problems of the least developed and landlocked countries among the developing countries. The United States supported the idea of special assistance for the least developed among the developing countries.

UNCTAD IV was held for 3 weeks in May 1976 in Nairobi. It was attended by the highest ranking U.S. delegation in UNCTAD history. Like its predecessors, UNCTAD IV was preceded by a meeting of the LDC's. This meeting was held in Manila under the aegis of the Group of 77, and over 100 developing countries participated in the meeting. The group drew up 17 demands that would restructure international trade, mitigate the debt burdens of the less developed countries, and improve commodity price stability. Most of the commodities cited are agricultural products.

The 17 demands were unacceptable to most developed countries. As an alternative, the United States presented a plan for an international resources bank that would meet the reciprocal needs of developing and industrialized countries. The proposal fell a few votes short of acceptance. In its place the conference adopted, over the opposition of many developed countries including the United States, a plan for an International Commodity Fund to create commodity buffer stocks aimed at dampening fluctuations in prices. The United States did not commit itself to participation in the proposed fund but it agreed to participate in preliminary discussions. The resolution on the fund included a timetable for its implementation. Preparatory meetings began their work September 1, 1976, and are scheduled to complete their work no later than February 1978. Commodity negotiations are to be concluded by the end of 1978. Financing for the International Commodity Fund operations would come from both producing and consuming countries, and OPEC countries are expected to contribute to the fund on behalf of producing developing countries. Commodities covered by the proposal include bananas, bauxite, cocoa, coffee, copper, cotton, jute, meat, phosphates, rubber, sugar, tea, hard fibers, and vegetable oils; other commodities could be added later.

UNCTAD meetings provide another forum in which the developing countries may exert pressure on the more developed countries for increased aid and better terms of trade. Since the economies of the developing countries continue to be principally agricultural, there are implications for agricultural policies for both less developed and developed countries. Resolutions passed in UNCTAD meetings largely reflect the views of delegates from developing countries, who represent a preponderance of the member countries.

UNCTAD's substantive committees and its Trade and Development Board (TDB) permit a continuing dialogue between developed and less developed countries on critical trade and development issues. UNCTAD and TDB thus represent an institutionalization of developing country efforts to secure more favorable terms of trade and a larger voice in the process by which international decisions are made affecting trade and development of the less developed countries.

New Development Dialogues

In recognition of the new economic power of the OPEC countries and the economic interdependence of industrialized and developing countries, a new series of intensive discussions was undertaken in 1976 outside the UN system. It was originally planned as a two-way dialogue between oil exporters and importers, but it was agreed to broaden the range of issues under the general heading of a Conference on International Economic Cooperation (CIEC) and to include representative governments from low-income developing countries as well as OPEC. The first meeting at the ministerial level was convened in December 1975. Four working commissions were established to deal with (1) development, (2) energy, (3) raw materials, and (4) finance. Issues of increasing food and agriculture production in developing countries were a major element in the commission on development, while trade in agricultural commodities was a major element in the raw materials commission.

The organization and operations of the conference were carefully worked out to reflect a balancing of interests, and the number of governments represented was kept low to facilitate direct discussions and negotiated conclusions. Twenty-seven countries were designated to participate in the CIEC, nine each from among the industrialized countries, the OPEC countries, and other developing countries. Each of the four commissions has a cochairman and a 15-country membership reflecting a balance of interests among the 10 developing and 5 industrialized countries represented on each. Most countries serve on more than one commission. A small *ad hoc* secretariat serves the conference and meetings are held in Paris.

Each of the four commissions works out its own agenda, and prepares staff papers on each subject. Each session of the conference lasts about a week. Proposals for policies and programs are usually made by one group of countries or another and these are the basis for intensive discussion.

During the first 6 months of periodic meetings, eight topics were discussed in the Development Commission: trade, balance of payments problems, food and agriculture, infrastructure, transfer of resources, industrialization and transfer of technology, investment, and special problems of the least developed, island, and landlocked countries. Although there were rigidities in the positions taken by each group of countries, the meetings provided candid exchanges, in the spirit apparent during the UN Seventh Special Session. A meeting of high officials was convened in July 1976 to assess progress and to consider a program of work for the next 6 months. That meeting did not reach agreement on some aspects of the agenda for the second half year's work but the sessions were continued in November 1976.

In the area of food and agriculture, the differences between industrialized and developing countries were less marked than on other topics. The principal points taken up in the first half of 1976 carried over to the second half. The topics on which concrete programs and policies are sought include (1) increasing agricultural production in developing countries—particularly foodstuffs, (2) improving supplies and prices of fertilizers for developing countries, (3) strengthening world food security, and (4) providing more adequate food aid. These topics have been discussed in other international forums, most notably the World Food Council and UNCTAD IV.

It remains to be seen whether the conference setting of intensive discussions among representative governments of OPEC, the industrialized countries, and the developing countries will lead to greater consensus than has emerged from other forums. Because the CIEC setting includes demands by the industrialized as well as the developing countries respecting energy and raw materials, some meeting of minds may be possible. In any event, the new forum and format, dealing with a broad range of economic problems and providing for intensive study and discussion, offer possibilities for negotiating differences not available in other international organizations. Moreover, there may be possibilities for delegating to existing institutions any operational programs that may be agreed upon; in that way, CIEC is expected to be phased out when its deliberations are concluded.

Food Production, Commercialization, and Rural Development

In addition to the new institutional arrangements that have affected international agricultural development efforts in recent years, there are several issues that are influencing the allocation of resources by the international organizations. These issues include rural development, population, environmental concerns, and interagency coordination for effective use of resources.

The stark need to increase food production in many developing countries has led to increased efforts in agriculture by international organizations. This has coincided with developing country aspirations to broaden their commercial agriculture for both domestic and export markets. Commercialization means modernization for most. These efforts arise out of a concern to generate employment as well as to increase output for market. The need to earn and save more foreign exchange is another factor; if LDC's can manufacture their own fertilizers and related farming inputs, and process more of the commodities they import and export, their foreign exchange balances can be improved. Still another factor is a growing recognition of the interrelatedness of agricultural and industrial development and the need to achieve a better balance between them.

Until the food crisis of 1973-74, FAO interest in forestry and fisheries rose steadily, and each was elevated to department status in the FAO. Both areas offer prospects for developing processing industries, to help developing nations earn and save foreign exchange. The IBRD and the IDB have put more emphasis on the development of livestock industries in Latin America and their loans have been concerned with export marketing as well as domestic production and consumption. A relatively new UN agency, the Industrial Development Organization (UNIDO), has responsibility for furthering industrialization in developing countries; and in the agricultural sector, UNIDO collaborates with FAO in supporting programs of agro-industries.

Despite the emphasis on agricultural commercialization and increasing food production, a second and somewhat conflicting emphasis on rural development has arisen among those concerned with social equity. The first

122

effort focuses on the productive capability of larger agricultural enterprises with their potential for profits and increased output; the second often focuses on smaller farmers and landless rural workers, and is concerned with their earnings and equity in the emergent commercial agricultural systems of the developing countries. While increased commercialization in agriculture may also lead to increased benefits for small farmers and rural workers, the record thus far indicates the need for special efforts to reach them.

The multilateral assistance agencies have recently begun to examine the problems of small landholders, and related equity considerations in their programs. Thus, the president of the World Bank Group, in his address to the Board of Governors on September 25, 1972, made the issue of social equity central to his observations about the development process. He noted that for some 40 percent of developing country populations, development is "not reaching them in any decisive degree. . .their countries are growing in gross economic terms but their individual lives are stagnating in human terms. . .the miracle of the Green Revolution may have arrived, but for the most part, the poor farmer has not been able to participate in it." In line with this point of view, IBRD has established a unit concerned with rural development to focus on what it might do to assist small farmers. A world conference on agrarian reform and integrated rural development is scheduled for 1979 under FAO auspices.

The dual objectives of encouraging the growth of a commercial agriculture and of obtaining greater equity for smaller farmers and landless farmworkers raise policy issues for the multilateral aid organizations and the governments of developing countries they assist. For the governments concerned there are questions of tradeoffs, such as ameliorating current deprivation among the rural poor versus stimulating more production and earnings for the economy generally. For multilateral organizations, similar tradeoff questions arise.

Where loans are made to smaller and less viable agricultural enterprises, the international finance agencies also face the problem of maintaining the quality of their loans (from a banking point of view). In designing projects and loans to reach smaller enterprises, there may need to be compromises with overall economic returns and with financial returns to individual entrepreneurs. And such loans may not provide rates of return as high as the international banks have had in the past. Seeking to reach more marginal groups within the economies of the developing countries (like helping the least developed countries) may create more work and higher administrative costs for the financial institution relative to the amount of the loan. Poorer operating ratios and higher operating costs may result. At issue is the portfolio "mix" as between projects which emphasize production and those which stress socioeconomic objectives.

World Agriculture, Population Growth, and the Environment

Rising concern about the environment in the councils and forums of international organizations is having an impact on programs for agricultural development. Three aspects of this emergent issue as it pertains to agriculture should be noted: (1) the grim war against hunger persists as the developing countries barely maintain food production at levels to keep up with their

123

burgeoning populations. If present trends persist, the shortfall in grains is expected to grow in developing countries from about 45 million tons in 1975 to over 95 million tons by 1985.[4] Much of this import requirement will occur in South Asia and sub-Sahara Africa where country earnings severely limit food purchases on the world's commercial markets. The outcome of the battle for survival in these countries is still uncertain. (2) As new lands are brought under the plow, natural resources such as soils, forests, and water supplies for rural areas are being depleted, upsetting ecological balances. Moreover, in some developing countries urbanization is using more and more cropland, thereby aggravating the problem of feeding urban populations. (3) High-yield technology is dependent on increased use of fertilizers, pesticides, and insecticides, which in turn may have deleterious side effects on waterways and wildlife.

Population

The Malthusian specter of populations growing more rapidly than the means to sustain them, which cast a shadow over many developing countries in 1965-66, still seems a menace in 1976. The fear that food supplies cannot keep pace with growing populations in these countries has been given added dimension by environmentalists and others concerned with the quality of human life. Hence, there has been a growing concern by organizations in the UN family to organize and stimulate efforts by member governments to acknowledge the problem of unchecked population growth and to undertake specific actions to arrest that growth rate. These efforts are of particular concern in those countries where pressure on the arable land is already severe and the trend lines of food production and population growth portend a grim confrontation in the near future.

A Fund for Population Activities (UNFPA) has been established as the central funding and principal coordinating mechanism for organizations within the UN. UNFPA finances projects related to every aspect of population and family planning—demography, education, research, advisory services, and training.

The 26th General Assembly in December 1970 gave added support to the fund by adopting a resolution that invited governments to make voluntary contributions to it and requested the UN Secretary General to improve its administrative machinery in order to accelerate the delivery of population assistance. In February 1971, the United States pledged to match contributions of other donors up to $15 million toward the 1971 goal of $25 to $30 million for the UNFPA. Forty-five other donor countries contributed over $14.5 million during the year, and the fund, with the U.S. matching contributions, thus received $29 million (44). By 1974, the United States was contributing some $20 million, with other donors adding $34 million for an operating program exceeding $50 million.

---

[4]Dale Hathaway, "Meeting Food Needs in the Developing World: The Location and Magnitude of the Task in the Next Decade." International Food Research Policy Institute, 1976.

124

Several organizations in the UN system concerned with food and agriculture have established units to study how their programs might include population considerations. Thus, FAO recently established a population unit to better relate some of FAO's work on supply and demand projections for food. An expanded plan of work on population questions was begun in 1973.

IBRD has also established a unit to study ways in which the Bank might appropriately finance activities in the population field. Currently, IBRD has cooperated with UNFPA on a major program in Indonesia; the family planning project is centered on the populous islands of Java and Bali. The IBRD is also cooperating with the Government of Sweden on jointly financing $21.2 million of a $31.8 million population project in two states of India. IBRD and UNFPA are also collaborating on a project in Malaysia to expand family planning into rural areas and to improve the effectiveness of that country's National Family Planning Board. During 1976, IBRD made its second loan to Jamaica in support of its population program.

Under UN sponsorship, a World Population Conference was held in Bucharest in August 1974. Among significant action proposals adopted by the conference are these:

• Governments should provide individuals the information and means for exercising the basic human right of spacing their children.

• Governments should include population policies and programs in their development planning.

• Reducing population growth and promoting socioeconomic development are mutually reinforcing and together lead to a higher quality of life.

Despite evidences of increased interest and involvement in population control problems, the multilateral assistance agencies have moved slowly and cautiously in this area.

The Human Environment

In June 1972, the United Nations convened a conference on the human environment in Stockholm. Divergent views as to the most urgent environmental problems were particularly marked between the less developed and the more developed countries. For the developing countries the most serious problem of the human environment was the persistent poverty of so many of their peoples. Moreover, they were concerned that the developed countries' preoccupation with environmental problems arising from industrialization and urbanization would deter efforts to modernize their own economies.

A UN panel of experts noted that environmental problems of developing countries may be categorized as follows: (1) those arising out of poverty (or the inadequacy of development), and (2) those that arise from the process of development itself. The report dealt primarily with environmental problems that might be alleviated by better planning and execution of development projects. In agriculture, the experts noted that traditional systems of agricultural production often were more devastating than modern

125

farm methods on soil productivity and on the ability of increasing populations to make a livelihood from the land. Nevertheless, they cautioned development planners and organizations giving aid to take environmental side effects into account in expanding the use of insecticides and pesticides, undertaking river basin development projects which change ecological patterns in the region, and instituting irrigation projects that carry the risk of salinization and waterlogging.[5]

Resolutions passed during the UN Conference in Stockholm bearing on agricultural development cited the need to:

- Strengthen work on conservation of genetic resources,
- Study environmental aspects of livestock development,
- Conduct studies on integrated pest control and reduction of harmful effect of agrochemicals,
- Assess the economic value of wildlife and monitor the effects of pollution on wildlife, and
- Conduct research and exchange information on forest fires, pests, and diseases.[6]

At issue in the debates on environmental problems in the developing countries is how external assistance may be allocated, and what kind of economies will emerge in the developing countries. Some environmentalists urge that many developing countries maintain basically agricultural economies organized to meet their food and employment needs and not patterned after the capital-intensive agro-industrial economies of the more developed countries (12, pp. 300-307). Leaders of some of the larger LDC's reject limitations on their development in the name of environmental considerations. They assert that the more developed countries are most responsible for polluting the environment and unduly utilizing world resources, and hence need to exercise the most restraint.[7]

The UN General Assembly, during its 27th session in October 1972, appointed a committee to draft a resolution on the question of institutional and financial arrangements for international environmental cooperation.[8] The United States served on the 11-member drafting committee which recommended, among other things, that the Assembly establish a Governing Council for Environmental Programs composed of 54 members elected by the

---

[5]"Development and Environment," a report submitted by a panel of experts convened by the Secretary-General of the UN Conference on the Human Environment, cited in Development Digest, Gordon Donald, ed., April 1972.

[6]Memorandum on "Implications of the Action Plan of the UN Conference on the Human Environment on FAO Programmes," submitted to the Fifty-Ninth Session of the FAO Council, Rome, November 1972.

[7]Statement delivered by the Brazilian representative to Committee II, XXVII Session of the General Assembly on agenda item 47, UN Conference on the Human Environment, Nov. 29, 1971, cited in Development Digest, Gordon Donald, ed., April 1972.

[8]Draft Resolution: Institutional and Financial Arrangement for International Environmental Cooperation, 27th Session, UN General Assembly, Oct. 16, 1972.

General Assembly for 3-year terms. This council and its small secretariat would provide leadership and coordination for UN programs and activities bearing on environmental problems. Special consideration is indicated to avoid having environmental considerations or costs inhibit development programs of the less developed countries. Reports would be made annually to the General Assembly through the Economic and Social Council. The costs of servicing the Governing Council and providing the small core secretariat would be borne by the regular UN budget. On the other hand, costs of operating the program would be covered by an Environmental Fund financed by voluntary contributions. Cooperation with member governments and indigenous nongovernment organizations concerned with problems of environment would be sought.

The Resolutions passed by the Conference on Human Environment and those of the General Assembly have led international organizations to evaluate some of their agricultural project requests in terms of environmental impact. The extent to which new environmental programs are undertaken and the extent to which present agricultural programs are affected will largely depend on the level of funding available to international organizations for this purpose. Moreover, today's basic food needs of the rural poor will weigh upon them more heavily than environmental considerations of another year. Some improvement in economic conditions as well as better understanding may be necessary to safeguard the environment.

Program Coordination and Effective Use of Resources

With the increased role of multilateral institutions in providing development assistance, the problem of coordination among organizations has grown more complex and compelling. While ultimate responsibility for country coordination rests with the recipient governments, the international organizations recognize that their available resources can be more usefully deployed if they take some measures to coordinate policies and programs. The principal multilateral assistance agencies have employed various means to coordinate their efforts and to deliver their program resources more effectively. They include country programing and sector analysis, as well as interagency consultations.

Country Programing and Sector Analysis

One way in which IBRD and FAO are seeking to improve deployment of resources for agricultural development is by conducting broad-gauged agricultural sector studies and relating these to the overall country economy and national development plans. The sector analyses provide a starting point for determining what projects are likely to have the greatest potential for contributing to the country's agricultural development. Such analyses can provide the international organizations with appropriate priority projects to support. FAO has also initiated a program of training in agricultural sector analysis to help officers concerned with development planning make the kinds of economic analyses needed to provide assistance agencies with the requisite information on costs and benefits of alternative projects.

127

The UNDP, following internal reviews, has taken steps to improve its coordinating efforts. The UN General Assembly, in its 25th session, approved proposals for UNDP to include country programing in its activities in order to link assistance with the objectives of individual country development plans. Country programing for agriculture has been carried on under joint UNDP/FAO country representatives who have responsibility for recommending specific development projects for UNDP/FAO approval. If the programing activities are placed within the framework of an FAO indicative plan for the country or the UNDP's 5-year aid plans, individual project proposals can be evaluated in terms of their contribution to the country's projected development (49).

Efforts at making country programing a useful tool for coordination and rationalization of external assistance raise several questions: How broad should the scope of programing activities be? Which international organizations should participate? Where should programing responsibility be placed—within the UN system or with some *ad hoc* consortium of bilateral and multilateral agencies? The issue transcends programs in the agricultural sector and touches on the overall development strategy of a country and the acceptance of that strategy by external assistance organizations. Despite gains in planning competency and increasing sophistication in the uses of development models and computers, few developing countries are prepared to make such comprehensive economic analyses and break them down to project size for possible inputs by the specialized agencies of the United Nations.

Interagency Coordination

International organizations providing assistance are increasing efforts to coordinate their activities where countries receive aid from several multilateral and bilateral agencies. The mechanism for such coordination, and the agency taking the lead in bringing it about, vary with the particular country situation. Consortia have made several attempts to coordinate development assistance activities. The first was the India Consortium sponsored by the World Bank in 1958. Two years later, the Bank sponsored a similar group in Pakistan. Following these examples OECD organized consortia in Greece and Turkey in 1962.

Fifteen other groups concerned with coordinating multilateral and bilateral aid efforts have been formed. IBRD has sponsored groups in Sri Lanka, Colombia, East Africa, Indonesia, Korea, Malaysia, Morocco, Nigeria, Peru, Sudan, Thailand, and Tunisia. During 1972, the World Bank participated in sessions with 10 of these countries dealing with development performance and prospects, and external capital requirements. The IMF sponsored a group in Ghana and the IDB organized a group for Ecuador.

These efforts at coordination have had mixed results; a number of the groups have ceased to function on a regular basis. According to OECD, a major problem lies in donor reluctance to endorse country plans and to relate their aid to local priorities (33; 1971, pp. 133-136). Another has been the different interests that each donor country brings to the consortium. These differences, both economic and political, influence the approach each favors and make agreements difficult to achieve.

While the consortia organized by IBRD actually pledge money, consultative groups which make no such commitment might find it easier to reach agreement on program issues. The Development Assistance Committee of OECD is a consultative group of donor countries which focuses on problems of particular countries from time to time, but does so without direct action by either donor or receiver country. According to OECD, however, consultative groups have often lacked some effectiveness because their views were not directly associated with those of the entities providing external capital assistance.

For a number of years, the Inter-American Committee on the Alliance for Progress (CIAP) provided technical and advisory reviews for donor agencies and development planners in the respective countries, and these reviews carried weight within the CIAP framework. The development agencies—IBRD, IDB, and USAID—worked together in the CIAP country reviews. But after a decade, the effectiveness of the process was questioned and new procedures for coordinating assistance in the Western Hemisphere are being explored.

Extensive coordination takes place among multilateral agencies (and with USAID and other major bilateral agencies) on a less formal basis than that of organized consortia or consultative groups or the contractual arrangements such as those between FAO and IBRD or FAO and IDB. For example, IBRD analyses of the economies of borrowing countries, its sector studies, and reports appraising IBRD and IDA projects are made available to organizations in the UN family and regional development banks. In turn, papers on country programing prepared by UNDP resident representatives are made available to country and regional officers in the international banks as well as appropriate agencies in the UN system.

As previously indicated, the World Food Council was established to coordinate the activities of the several international organizations concerned with food and agriculture development. The council also looks at the relationships among such factors as programs and policies of developing countries; kinds and levels of assistance by bilateral and multilateral development agencies; production, distribution, and consumption of food; and questions of nutrition among different population groups. In Latin America, the newly established International Group for Agriculture Development, associated with the Inter-American Development Bank, also seeks a coordinating role. Some suggest that the FAO, since it is the principal UN agency involved and has the broadest range of agricultural development activities, should also have a coordinating function. Others feel that there may be too many international organizations wanting to coordinate and that their effect is to pyramid bureaucracies. At issue is who will control and direct the flow of resources for food and agricultural development purposes. Different international organizations with separate governing bodies are likely to establish different criteria for disbursing aid.

In some developing countries, the question is in part answered by their preference for a transfer of resources with a minimum of strings and involvement by donor institutions in the way the resources are utilized. For them the question is less a matter of efficient use of development resources than political independence in the deployment of external transfers. Hence, efforts to bring about such transfers in a mechanical fashion, through a fixed proportion of GNP or through commodity agreements which assure export earnings for the developing countries, are now being pushed by many of them. Similarly, a restructuring of the UN system to make it a more effective economic development instrument for the developing country majority in the General Assembly would shift more control over development resources into their hands.

Restructuring the UN System

In response to suggestions and urgings by member governments, the UN Secretary General, in the fall of 1974, appointed a high-level group of 25 experts to study the UN system as it pertained to economic cooperation and development, and to report their findings and recommendations to him. The group of experts, from different countries but appointed in their personal capacity, presented their conclusions in May 1975. The report, A New United Nations Structure for Global Economic Cooperation, proposed sweeping changes in the economic activities of the UN and in the institutional relationships of its associated agencies.

Then, an omnibus resolution of the Seventh Special Session of the UN General Assembly, September 1975, referred to restructuring the "economic and social sectors of the UN system." The Secretary General was asked to appoint an Ad Hoc Committee to study the issues of restructuring the UN system, taking into account the report of the expert group, as well as UNGA resolutions on a new international economic order and discussions in other relevant UN bodies. In June 1976, the Ad Hoc Committee made its report.

One important recommendation of the Ad Hoc Committee was that the Economic and Social Council of the UN, the highest deliberative body in these areas of UN activity, establish small consultative groups that would endeavor over a 1- to 2-year period to work out solutions between developing and developed countries on key economic issues. Some felt that complex or controversial issues reviewed continually by such groups would more likely be resolved in this fashion than during brief interactions between nations in large bodies which meet once or twice yearly. Both the developed and less developed countries would have to agree on topics to be reviewed by such groups and they would apparently function much like the recently established CIEC groups.

Other actions tentatively recommended by the Ad Hoc Committee included one which would strengthen relations between the regional commissions and the organizations of the UN system, particularly UNDP. Regional commissions would participate in planning and implementing relevant regional, subregional, and interregional projects financed by UNDP when requested by the countries concerned and recommended by the administrator of UNDP. This would decentralize UNDP decisionmaking and place more control close to the developing countries where the programs were carried out.

Other recommendations call for an overall review of operational activities throughout the UN system, and the establishment of a number of new positions, including the post of Director General for Development and

Economic Policy. New personnel policies advocated by the Ad Hoc Committee would strengthen the requirement for competitive recruitment in the International Civil Service of the United Nations.

Further discussions of the Ad Hoc Committee proposals continued through 1976, with referrals of proposals to the General Assembly in the September-December 1976 session.

One result of the changes proposed by the Ad Hoc Committee would be to strengthen the role of the General Assembly with respect to the specialized agencies and other parts of the UN system. While the move might improve coordination of social and economic development activities by UN agencies, it could also enhance developing country influence in such activities since they have preponderant voting power in the General Assembly. The specialized agencies and other autonomous bodies of the United Nations registered reservations on some of the coordination plans as discussed early in 1976. Since each of the specialized agencies has its own governing bodies made up of member nations, it is not clear how these bodies and principal donor governments would respond to a reduction in operating autonomy.

* * * * * *

This survey of multilateral assistance reflects not only an increasing flow of resources for agricultural development, but a growing difference between donor and recipient countries toward the role of international agencies in the overall development process of which agriculture is a major part. Some of this difference stems from the change in membership of UN organizations in the past decade, and the resulting shift in voting power to the less developed countries. And developing countries are seeking to use their new UN power to transform international agencies from deliberative to quasi-legislative bodies for achieving significant changes in the international economic system—with a larger share of the benefits accruing to them. International organizations are seeking to become centers for harmonizing the actions of nations; this process does not always coincide with U.S. views on the objectives sought or the methods of attaining them. From the U.S. point of view, this changing relationship will require some changes in how it operates in the international organizations. Accustomed to a successful leadership role, the United States may turn more frequently to lesser involvement, and abstain from voting on important issues. But this reaction, and the failure of the United States to fully employ its leadership capacities may in turn lead to even more diffusion of purpose and greater departures from the U.S. point of view in the priorities pursued by the multilateral agencies. If the downward spiral is to be avoided, the United States may need to commit itself to greater rather than less participation in international organizations and to more positive, purposeful involvement in their work programs and policy proposals.

BIBLIOGRAPHY OF SOURCE MATERIALS
AND REFERENCES CITED

(1) African Development Bank
Report to the Directors. ADB/BC/XII/2. Abidjan, Ivory Coast, Dec. 1975.

(2) _____
African Development Fund, Report on Third Annual Meeting. ADF/BG/III/2. Abidjan, Ivory Coast, Sept. 1975.

(3) Armstrong, Hamilton Fish
"Isolated America," Foreign Affairs, Oct. 1972.

(4) Asian Development Bank
Background Information and Materials Relating to Membership of the United States. Jan. 1968.

(5) _____.
Annual Reports, 1971, 1974, 1975.

(6) _____
ADB Quarterly Review. Jan. 1976.

(7) Baum, Warren C.
"The Project Cycle," Finance and Development. Washington, D.C., International Monetary Fund, June 1970.

(8) Consultative Group on Food Production and Investment
Further Analysis of Resource Flows in Agriculture. Doc. D, prepared for the Third Meeting of CGFPI, Sept. 22-24, 1976. Washington, D.C.

(9) Consultative Group on International Agricultural Research
International Research in Agriculture. New York, 1974.

(10) Development Coordination Committee
Development Issues: U.S. Actions Affecting the Development of Low Income Countries. First and Second Annual Reports of the President, transmitted to Congress May 1975 and May 1976.

(11) Economic Commission for Africa
African Development Bank: Its Functions and Purposes. Abidjan, Ivory Coast, 1964.

(12) Ehrlich, Paul and Anne Erlich
Population, Resources, Environment. San Francisco, W.H. Freeman Co., 1970.

(13) Finkelstein, Lawrence
"International Cooperation in a Changing World," International Organizations, Summer 1969.

(14) Food and Agriculture Organization of the United Nations
Agricultural Development, A Review of FAO's Field Activities. Basic Study No. 23. Rome, 1970.

(15) _____
FAO/Government Cooperative Program. FAO Doc. DDA: Misc/70/2 Rome, March 20, 1970.

(16) _____
FAO-Industry Cooperative Program. Rome, 1970.

(17) _____
World Food Program. Second ed. Rome, 1971.

(18) _____
World Food Program, Report of the Governmental Committee, 28th Session. FR/B76. Rome Sept.-Oct. 1975.

(19) _____
Review of Field Programs, 1972-1973. C 73/4. Aug. 1973, and Review of Field Programs, 1974-1975. C 75/4. Aug. 1975, Rome.

(20) _____
Streamlining FAO, Report by the FAO Director General to the 59th Session of the FAO Council. Rome, Nov. 1972.

(21) _____
FAO in 1975. Rome, 1976.

(22) Haberler, Gottfried
"International Trade and Development," in Reshaping the World Economy, John Pincus, ed. New York, Prentice Hall, 1968.

(23) Inter-American Development Bank
Annual Reports, 1972, 1973, 1974, 1975. Washington, D.C.

(24) _____
Fifteen Years of Activities, 1960-1974. Washington, D.C., March 1975.

(25) _____
Participation of the Bank in the Development of Agriculture in Latin America. Washington, D.C., April 1976.

(26) _____
Structure, Resources, Operations. Washington, D.C., July 1972.

(27) Inter-American Institute of Agricultural Sciences
1975-76 Budget, and Annual Report, 1975-76. San Jose, Costa Rica.

(28) International Food Policy Research Institute
Meeting Food Needs in the Developing World. Washington, D.C., 1976.

(29) Johnson, Harry
"Trade Preferences and Developing Nations," in Reshaping the World Economy, John Pincus, ed. New York, Prentice Hall, 1968.

(30) The National Advisory Council on Monetary and Financial Policies
International Finance, Annual Report to the President, July 1, 1974 to June 30, 1975. Washington, D.C., Dec. 1975.

(31) _____
Communication from the Secretary of the Treasury. A Special Report from the National Advisory Council on the Proposed Increase in the Capital Resources of the International Finance Corporation, June 14, 1976. Washington, D.C.

(32) Organization for Economic Cooperation and Development
Evaluation and Future Outlook for Aid to Agricultural Development in Developing Countries and for Food Aid. DAC (76)1. Paris, Feb. 6, 1976.

(33) _____
Development Assistance Review(s). Paris, 1969, 1971.

(34) _____
Development Cooperation, 1973, 1975.

(35) _____
"OPEC Countries as AID Donors, 1974-1975," The OECD Observer, No. 79/Jan.-Feb. 1976, p. 5.

(36) Maynes, Charles W.
"A UN Policy for the Next Administration," Foreign Affairs, July 1976.

(37) Peterson, Rudolph
U.S. Foreign Assistance in the 1970's. Report to the President of the United States. 1970.

(38) Phillips, Ralph W.
FAO, its Organization and Work and U.S. Participation. U.S. Dept. Agr., 1969.

(39) Prebish, Raul
Towards a New Trade Policy for Development. UN Conference on Trade and Development, 1964.

(40) _____
Change and Development. Inter-American Development Bank, July 1970.

(41) Scopes, Sir Leonard
Report on Country Programming and After. U.N. Joint Inspection Unit Report, Fifty-Ninth Session of the FAO Council. Rome, Nov. 1972.

(42) Society for International Development
Summary of Major International Development Reports. July 1971.

(43) U.S. Department of Agriculture, Economic Research Service
The World Food Situation and Prospects to 1985. Dec. 1974.

(44) U.S. Department of State
U.S. Participation in the U.N., Reports by the President to the Congress for the Years 1971, 1972, and 1973.

(45) U.S. Department of State, Agency for International Development
Summary of Ongoing Research and Technical Assistance Projects in Agriculture. Sponsored by the Office of Agriculture, Bureau for Technical Assistance. 1975.

(46) U.S. Senate Staff Report, prepared for the Select Committee on Nutrition and Human Needs
The United States, FAO and World Food Politics: U.S. Relations with an International Food Organization. Washington, D.C., 1976.

(47) United Nations
Continuity and Change—Development at Mid-Decade. New York, 1975.

(48) United Nations
Report of World Food Conference. E/Conf. 65/20. New York, spring 1975.

(49) United Nations Development Program
The Administrator Reports (Annual Report of the UNDP). New York, 1974 and 1975.

(50) White, John
Regional Development Banks: The Asian, African, and Inter-American Development Banks. New York, Praeger, 1972.

(51) Williams, Maurice J.
"The Aid Programs of OPEC Countries," Foreign Affairs, January 1976, Vol. 54, No. 2.

(52) World Bank
Annual Reports. Washington, D.C., 1970, 1972, 1973, 1974, 1975, 1976.

(53) _____
Address to the Board of Governors, Robert S. McNamara, President, World Bank Group. Washington, D.C., Sept. 1, 1975.

(54) _____
Economic Development Institute. 1972.

(55) _____
International Finance Corporation Annual Reports. Washington, D.C., 1973, 1974, 1975.

(56) _____
World Bank Operations: Sectoral Programs and Policies. Baltimore, Johns Hopkins Univ. Press, 1972.

(57) _____
Partners in Development. Report of the World Bank Commission on International Development, Lester B. Pearson, Chairman. New York, Praeger, Sept. 1969.

(58) _____
Report: News of the World Bank Group, Sept.-Oct. 1974 (bimonthly serial). Washington, D.C.

(59) _____
World Bank Research Program, Abstracts of Current Studies. Oct. 1975.

(60) _____
Rural Development, Sector Policy Paper. Feb. 1975.

CPSIA information can be obtained
at www.ICGtesting.com
Printed in the USA
BVHW071119291118
534321BV00014B/627/P